Teach us to Pray

Biblical Curriculum on Prayer

PRAYERFUL PUBLISHING

Student Personal Study Guide

Kingdom Builders

TEACH US TO PRAY
Student Personal Study Guide

Copyright © 2019 Dale Roy Erickson

ISBN 978-0-9884145-6-3
All Rights Reserved
Published by Prayerful Publishing, Inc., Meridian, Idaho, USA
www.prayerfulpublishing.com

"Scripture taken from the NEW AMERICAN STANDARD BIBLE®, Copyright © 1960, 1962, 1963, 1968, 1971, 1972, 1973, 1975, 1977, 1995 by The Lockman Foundation. Used by permission. www.Lockman.org"
Scripture taken from the HOLY BIBLE, NEW INTERNATIONAL VERSION® NIV®. Copyright © 1973, 1978, 1984 by International Bible Society ®. Used by permission of International Bible Society®.
All rights reserved worldwide.
Scripture taken from the New King James Version, copyright © 1979, 1980, 1982 by Thomas Nelson, Inc. Used by permission. All rights reserved.
Scripture quotations are taken from the Holy Bible, New Living Translation, copyright © 1996, 2004, 2007, © by Tyndale House foundation.
Used by permission of Tyndale House Publishers, Inc., Carol Stream, Illinois 60188. All rights reserved.

All rights reserved. No part of this book or MP3 audio files may be reproduced in any form without permission in writing from the publisher. No part of this publication may be reproduced in any form, stored in any retrieval system, posted on any website, or transmitted in any form or by any means – digital, electronic, scanning, photocopy, recording, or otherwise – without written permission from the author, except for brief quotations printed in reviews and articles, with accreditation.

Cover page photos and some internal photos are provided by and used with the permission of Blair Turner. You can view more of his exceptional work at www.baravisuals.weebly.com.

Prayerful Publishing, Inc. is a non-profit 501(c)(3) ministry dedicated to providing contemporary Biblical tools on the Christian discipline of prayer for the next generation.

Teach us to Pray

Acknowledgements

To the only true God and His Son, Jesus, who brings us grace, forgiveness and life; Connie Erickson, who has stood with me through all of life's adventures; Larry Patrick for his friendship, insight, encouragement and creative graphic design; Blair Turner for his terrific pictures used on the covers and throughout the books; Errol Lester for his magnificent narration; Jim Peterson and Bob Hutchings for their meticulous audio mix of the MP3 files; the Prayerful Publishing Board of Directors for their prayers, wisdom and support; Orval Mauldin for his gracious and painstaking editing; and to the host of people who challenged us to keep pressing on to the finish line. It's not over yet, and the best is yet to come.

Preface

The **Teach Us To Pray** curriculum is structured upon the various elements of prayer found in the *Lord's Prayer*. This Student Personal Study Guide is part of a multi-platform curriculum designed to help young people grow in their connection with God. The 35-lesson curriculum includes 35 short stories, a PDF handbook page that provides seven thoughts on prayer with the supporting Scripture for each lesson (a total of 245 prompts), this active participation Student Personal Study Guide, a Teacher's Manual with guidelines for teaching the lessons, a session planning sheet for each lesson, additional teacher resources, and of course, tests for each unit.

The curriculum is designed for the following possible settings: release time courses for public schools, middle school and high school youth groups, home school, Christian schools, and the training of indigenous Christian leaders.

About the Author

Dale Roy Erickson understands and lives out the importance of prayer in his individual life and in the corporate life of the church. He is established as a gifted and creative teacher who carefully studies and presents the truth of God's Word. Pastor Dale has had successful involvement in every facet of church ministry in the United States and Canada including children's, youth, adult, small group, and counseling. He has served on the national Christian education committee of the Christian & Missionary Alliance in Canada and traveled extensively across the Unites States as a field service representative specializing in youth and Christian education. He has taught release time for public high school classes for over 5 years. He serves as an example of godly living in his marriage, family, financial and personal life. It is his prayer that this curriculum will bring glory to God and provide insight for the prayer lives of many young people.

How to use this Study

The Student Personal Study Guide is one part of the multi-platform **Teach Us To Pray** curriculum. Other vital elements include: Teacher's Manual, Session outlines and Prompts handbook, **Heaven Help Us** short stories, and additional teacher resources.

You can order these resources at www.prayerfulpublishing.com

Print or MP3

App or PDF

Print or MP3

There is a well known saying that should be changed. "Why do you believe that a small group of dedicated people can change the world? Answer: "Because it is the only thing that ever has."

Revised version: "Why do you believe that a small group of dedicated people on their knees can change the world?" Answer: "Because that is the way God chooses to work!"

Acts 1:14 They all met together continually for prayer, along with Mary the mother of Jesus, several other women, and the brothers of Jesus. NLT

Prayer Prompts Handbook Print or PDF

www.prayerfulpublishing.com

Teach us to Pray
Contents:

UNIT 4: Kingdom Builders – *Approach with Meekness*
- Lesson 13: Gratitude 7
- Lesson 14: Humility 11
- Lesson 15: Grace 17
- Lesson 16: Faith 23
- Lesson 17: Joy 27

UNIT 5: Kingdom Builders – *Approach with Devotion*
- Lesson 18: Fellowship 32
- Lesson 19: Submission 36
- Lesson 20: Abiding 43

UNIT 6: Kingdom Builders – *Approach with Assurance*
- Lesson 21: Persistence 48
- Lesson 22: Petition/Provision 58
- Lesson 23: Shelter 64

UNIT 7: Kingdom Builders – *Approach with Compassion*
- Lesson 24: Mercy 70
- Lesson 25: Forgiveness 73

PRAYERFUL PUBLISHING

Student Personal Study Guide

Teach us to Pray
A note from the Author

I would like to share a little of my heart with you before we begin this journey.

I am convinced that there is nothing of greater value than helping you connect with God.

Asaph captured my motivations quite well in **Psalm 78:1-4 NLT**

> *"O my people, listen to my instructions.*

(I don't want you to just listen. I want you to get involved in every way.)

> *Open your ears to what I am saying, for I will speak to you in a parable.*

(OK I will use YouTube videos more than parables.)

> *I will teach you hidden lessons from our past – stories we have heard and known,*

(I will use MP3 audio files for our stories.)

> *stories our ancestors handed down to us. We will not hide these truths from our children;*

(Compared to you I am ancient, but I am not one of your ancestors.)

> *We will tell the next generation* (presumably that's YOU) *about the glorious deeds of the Lord, about his power, and his mighty wonders."*

So I invite you to open your hearts in the hope of catching a glimpse of His glorious deeds, His power and His mighty wonders!

– Dale

Approach with Meekness

Lesson 13: Gratitude - In everything give thanks

Perspective makes all the difference in the world.

Perspective makes all the difference in setting the right agenda or choosing a new direction. If you have ever flown in a plane, you very likely gained a new perspective on what life is like on the ground. A series of grain fields look very similar from ground level, but from the air they become an amazing patchwork of color. The Rocky Mountains look massive and majestic from the valley floor, but from 30,000 feet they have the appearance of waves on a lake. The Grand Canyon is a sight that will always exceed expectations and give people a new sense of humility, but if only seen once from high altitude, you might describe it like a rain gulley.

The first pictures of planet earth from outer space helped humanity gain a new point of view for our countries and the world. The further we went into outer space, the smaller our little world became. Our reach outward into the universe also shaped our view of ourselves. For some, it made us realize how very special and unique this world really is. For others, it spawned dreams of other planets that might share our rare position amongst the stars.

https://lupitanews.com/earth_and_limb_m11992915641_color_2stretch_mask/

When you consider the perspective of the God who spoke the stars into existence and called each one by name, you might be tempted to think that He would view us like grasshoppers or something even less significant. Fortunately, God's Word tells us just the opposite. He describes mankind as the highlight of His creation (Psalm 8:3-6), and not only knows each of us by name (Jeremiah 1:5), but deeply loves us (Jeremiah 31:3), and calls us His friend (John 15:15).

Our perspective is shaped by so many things. We have learned that birth order can influence how we view and interact with our world. The family heritage and cultural/societal values have a significant impact on our world view. Our religious traditions and morals have a powerful effect on our motivations. The part of the world, or even the particular sub-culture of our birth place, will have an impact on the way we think and the choices we make. The list could go on and on, but for today's lesson we will focus on only one element of our place in the world. We will be taking a look at the place where we were raised in comparison to an overview of the entire world.

You will find the statistics which were compiled by: 2016 - Fritz Erickson, Provost and Vice President for Academic Affairs, Ferris State University (Formerly Dean of Professional and Graduate Studies, University of Wisconsin - Green Bay) and John A. Vonk, University of Northern Colorado, 2006; Returning Peace Corps Volunteers of Madison Wisconsin, *Unheard Voices: Celebrating Cultures from the Developing World*, 1992; Donella H. Meadows, *The Global Citizen*, May 31, 1990 at http://www.100people.org/statistics_100stats.php?section=statistics.

What influences the way you view your place in the world?

Find the answers to this exercise at:
http://www.100people.org/statistics_100stats.php?section=statistics

1. In the home where you were raised _____% were female and _____% were male.
If the World were 100 PEOPLE: _____ are Female _____ are Male
How does that influence the way you view your place in the world? _____
_____
_____

2. In the home you live in right now, what percentage of the people are:
_____% Asian _____% African _____% European _____% American
If the World were 100 PEOPLE:
____ would be Asian ____ would be European ____ would be African ____ would be American
How does that influence the way you view your place in the world? _____
_____
_____

3. In the home you live in right now, what percentage are:
_____% Christian _____% Muslim _____% not religious or not aligned with a particular faith
_____% Hindu _____% Buddhist _____% other religions
If the World were 100 PEOPLE:
_____ would be Christian _____ would be Muslim _____ would be Hindu
_____ would be Buddhist _____ other religions _____ would be not religious or not aligned
How does that influence the way you view your place in the world? _____
_____
_____

4. In the home you or your extended family live in, what percentage of the people speak:
_____% Chinese _____% Spanish _____% English _____% Hindi _____% Arabic
_____% Other language
If the World were 100 PEOPLE:
_____ would speak Chinese _____ would speak Spanish _____ would speak English
_____ would speak Hindi _____ Arabic _____ would speak other languages
How does that influence the way you view your place in the world? _____
_____
_____

5. In the home live in or in your extended family, what percentage would be literate? _____%

If the World were 100 PEOPLE: _____ could read   _____ could not read

How does that influence the way you view your place in the world? _____
_____
_____

6. What percentage of your immediate or extended family have a college degree? _____%

If the World were 100 PEOPLE: _____ would have a College degree

How does that influence the way you view your place in the world? _____
_____
_____

7. What percentage of the people you know do not have access to the internet? _____%

If the World were 100 PEOPLE: _____ would have an internet connection

How does that influence the way you view your place in the world? _____
_____
_____

8. What percentage of your immediate or extended family have somewhere to live? _____%

If the World were 100 PEOPLE:

_____ would have somewhere to live   _____ would not have somewhere to live

How does that influence the way you view your place in the world? _____
_____
_____

9. What percentage of the people you know (friends and family) don't have enough to eat? _____%

If the World were 100 PEOPLE:

_____ would have enough to eat   _____ would not have enough to eat

How does that influence the way you view your place in the world? _____
_____
_____

10. What percentage of the people you know (friends and family) have safe drinking water? _____%

If the World were 100 PEOPLE:

_____ would have safe drinking water   _____ would not have safe drinking water

How does that influence the way you view your place in the world? _____
_____
_____

With these statistics in mind, make a list of things that you are grateful for in "your world."

___

Other than the things that are based on those statistics, how many other things are you grateful for in your world?

___

Read Lesson 13 Short Story: HHU Vol. 2 - Gratitude

- Memory Verse -

Let the words of my mouth and the meditation of my heart Be acceptable in Your sight, O LORD, my rock and my Redeemer.
Psalm 19:14 NASB

Approach with Meekness

Lesson 14: Humility - It's not thinking less of yourself

> We often think that we can tell if a person is proud or humble, but... we can be mistaken.

One of the elements of Jesus' kingdom coming to earth and being established in our hearts is found in the character trait of **humility**. It is clear that Jesus has set the example for us. Philippians 2:8 tells us that Jesus humbled himself. Jesus challenged us in Matthew 11:29 NASB: "*Take My yoke upon you and learn from Me, for I am gentle and humble in heart, and YOU WILL FIND REST FOR YOUR SOULS."*

According to the Bible, the first step in national restoration is humbling ourselves. 2 Chronicles 7:14 NIV says: "*If my people, who are called by my name, will humble themselves and pray and seek my face and turn from their wicked ways, then I will hear from heaven, and I will forgive their sin and will heal their land.*"

How exactly do we accomplish that? Humility and its antonym, **pride**, are often identified by peoples' actions and attitudes. While we often think that we can tell if a person is proud or humble, we can be mistaken. Since these qualities are a matter of the heart, only God knows the complete answer.

Since that it true, how can God challenge us to humble ourselves as He does in James 4:10 NASB which says: "*Humble yourselves in the presence of the Lord, and He will exalt you.*" James 4:6 NASB says: "*But He gives a greater grace. Therefore it says, 'GOD IS OPPOSED TO THE PROUD, BUT GIVES GRACE TO THE HUMBLE.'* " We certainly don't want God opposed to us, so let's learn more about what pride and humility might involve.

There are many elements to this character trait, and we might gain insight by seeing how it worked out in the lives of Joseph and his brothers.

Elements of the character trait Humility...

1. Genesis 37:3-4 **Coat of many colors** – Jacob (Israel) loved Joseph more than his other sons, and demonstrated this by making him a special coat that set him apart (i.e. more loved) from the others. How could that possibly lead to a pride or humility issue in Joseph's life?

_____
_____
_____

2. Genesis 37:5-11 **Joseph's dreams** – Joseph had two dreams that represented his family doing homage to him (i.e. honoring him). How could that possibly lead to a pride or humility issue in Joseph's life? How did his "sharing" about his dream possibly demonstrate either pride or humility? What are some responses that people have when someone else rises in stature? What does that response say about their predisposition to either pride or humility?

_____
_____
_____

3. Genesis 37:18-21 **Ruben plans to rescue Joseph** – Ruben was the first born of the sons, and as such would normally (in that culture) be the one in the lead when Jacob wasn't present. In your opinion, does his plan to rescue Joseph reflect more of a "responsibility" motive, a "humility" motive or a "compassion" motive? What does this plan reflect about an understanding of accountability (humility) before God or Jacob?

_____
_____
_____

4. Genesis 37:23-26 **Judah's profit scheme** – Judah presents a plan where the brothers could profit from their plans for Joseph. Does this plan reflect an arrogance (pride) about accountability (or lack thereof) before God?

_____
_____
_____

5. Genesis 37:27-28 **Joseph sold into slavery** – Having his brothers sell him as a slave may have presented Joseph with an opportunity to learn humility, or left him bitter. Which do you think he chose?

_____
_____
_____

6. Genesis 37:29-34 **Ruben's cover up** – Ruben lies to his father about what happened and covers it up. What does this plan reflect about an understanding of accountability (humility/pride) before God or Jacob?

_____
_____
_____

7. Genesis 39:1-3 **Joseph's skill recognized** – Do you think that when Joseph was placed in charge of the household he became proud or remained humble? What makes you believe that?

_____
_____
_____

8. Genesis 39:7-20 **Joseph falsely accused** – Do you think that Joseph's response reflected pride or humility when he was enticed and then falsely accused of rape?

_____
_____
_____

9. Genesis 39:21-23 **Joseph in charge of jail** – Do you think that Joseph being placed in charge of the jail presented an opportunity that could lead to pride or humility? What makes you believe that?

_____
_____
_____
_____
_____
_____

Teach Us To Pray I © 2019 I Prayerful Publishing Inc. I www.prayerfulpublishing.com I All Rights Reserved

10. Genesis 41:14-16; 33-41 **Joseph 2nd over Egypt** – Do you think that Joseph being in charge of all Egypt (excluding Pharaoh's authority) presented an opportunity that could lead to pride or humility? What makes you believe that?

_____
_____
_____

11. Genesis 42:1-8; 17 **Brothers bow down** – Do you think that his brothers bowing down before Joseph presented him with an opportunity for pride or humility? Did his brothers bowing down before Joseph present them with an opportunity for pride or humility? What makes you believe that?

_____
_____
_____

12. Genesis 42:18-24 **Simeon put in jail** – Do you think the brothers admitting their guilt helped shape Joseph's response? Why or why not? Do you think Ruben admitting their guilt represented humility on their part? Why or why not? Do you think Ruben's admission of guilt had anything to do with his being chosen as the one placed in prison? Do you think Ruben being the eldest brother when Joseph was sold into slavery had anything to do with his being chosen as the one placed in prison?

_____
_____
_____

13. Genesis 43:26-34 **Benjamin honored** – Benjamin was honored by being given a portion of food that was five times greater than his brothers. Do you think that could have made them jealous? How is jealousy related to pride or humility?

_____
_____
_____

14. Genesis 44:16-18; 32-34 **Judah's recompense** – Do you think that Judah being in a position of taking on responsibility for Benjamin's penalty was unrelated to his scheme of profiting from Joseph's sale as a slave? How are they similar? How are they different? What does his taking responsibility reveal in the issue of pride, humility, and selfishness in Judah's life?

_____
_____

15. Genesis 45:1-5; 50:15, 19-21 **Joseph's response** – In Joseph's mind, who was most responsible for the injustices done to him? What does his view in this matter teach us about what might be involved in "humbling ourselves"?

_____
_____
_____

There is one more poignant example of God warning someone about the dangers of pride. Nebuchadnezzar found God opposing him because of his pride. When he humbled himself, God restored him to his original position. That is found in Daniel 4:1-6; 27-37 NASB.

Nebuchadnezzar acknowledges that God is the ruler of all mankind.

Nebuchadnezzar, the king to all the peoples, nations, and *men of every* language that live in all the earth: "May your peace abound! It has seemed good to me to declare the signs and wonders which the Most High God has done for me."

"How great are His signs and how mighty are His wonders! His kingdom is an everlasting kingdom and His dominion is from generation to generation."

Nebuchadnezzar prospers and is warned about the dangers of pride through a dream.

I, Nebuchadnezzar was at ease in my house and flourishing in my palace. I saw a dream and it made me fearful; and *these* fantasies *as I lay* on my bed, and the visions in my mind, kept alarming me. So I gave orders to bring into my presence all the wise men of Babylon, that they might make known to me the interpretation of the dream.

Therefore, O king, may my advice be pleasing to you: break away now from your sins by *doing* righteousness and from your iniquities by showing mercy to *the* poor, in case there may be a prolonging of your prosperity. All *this* happened to Nebuchadnezzar the king.

Nebuchadnezzar ignores the warning and is lifted up in pride. He reaps the consequences.

Twelve months later he was walking on the *roof of* the royal palace of Babylon. The king reflected and said, "Is this not Babylon the great, which I myself have built as a royal residence by the might of my power and for the glory of my majesty?" While the word *was* in the king's mouth, a voice came from heaven, *saying*, 'King Nebuchadnezzar, to you it is declared: sovereignty has been removed from you, and you will be driven away from mankind, and your dwelling place *will be* with the beasts of the field. You will be given grass to eat like cattle, and seven periods of time will pass over you until you recognize that the Most High is ruler over the realm of mankind and bestows it on whomever He wishes.' Immediately the word concerning Nebuchadnezzar was fulfilled; and he was driven away from mankind and began eating grass like cattle, and his body was drenched with the dew of heaven until his hair had grown like eagles' *feathers* and his nails like birds' *claws*.

Nebuchadnezzar humbles himself, exalts God and is restored

"But at the end of that period, I, Nebuchadnezzar, raised my eyes toward heaven and my reason returned to me, and I blessed the Most High and praised and honored Him who lives forever;

For His dominion is an everlasting dominion,
And His kingdom endures from generation to generation.
All the inhabitants of the earth are accounted as nothing,
But He does according to His will in the host of heaven
And among the inhabitants of earth;
And no one can ward off His hand
Or say to Him, 'What have You done?'

At that time my reason returned to me. And my majesty and splendor were restored to me for the glory of my kingdom, and my counselors and my nobles began seeking me out; so I was reestablished in my sovereignty, and surpassing greatness was added to me. Now I, Nebuchadnezzar, praise, exalt and honor the King of heaven, for all His works are true and His ways just, and He is able to humble those who walk in pride."

Rewrite Nebuchadnezzar's exaltation of God in your own words:

_____
_____
_____
_____
_____

Read Lesson 14 Short Story: HHU Vol. 2 - Autonomous

- Memory Verse -

If My people who are called by My name will humble themselves, and pray and seek My face, and turn from their wicked ways, then I will hear from heaven, and will forgive their sin and heal their land. 2 Chronicles 7:14 NKJV

Approach with Meekness

Lesson 15: Grace - Finding grace and grace finding you

Use it or lose it but don't abuse it!

"I can't believe it! I got off with just a warning! The police had me dead to rights." "How'd you pull that off? My dad gets busted every time he gets pulled over. What happened?" "Well, I shouldn't even have been driving. I didn't have my motorcycle endorsement yet. I had just bought the bike from a friend and I just couldn't wait to drive it. To top that off, I was driving at night and the bike's headlight didn't work! I saw a car creeping up on me on the highway and I wasn't going to let them get by me... so I sped up to keep them from passing. I had no idea that it was a police officer until they pulled up right beside me and THEN turned on the lights. You know what that policeman did? He told me that it was too dangerous to drive home without lights and had me follow him until I got back home." "Amazing... for real?"

Noah found grace in the eyes of the Lord. Have you ever been there? Judgment is coming... in fact it's overdue and you deserve to have the book thrown at you. Was that the case for Noah? God looked things over and regretted that He had made man. Not my words. Those are God's words. Genesis 6:6 *"The LORD regretted that he had made human beings on the earth, and his heart was deeply troubled."* NIV

Don't stop reading there! God decided to take action and His actions included Noah. The next two verses reveal His plan and that plan involved grace. Genesis 6:7-8 *"So the LORD said, 'I will destroy man whom I have created from the face of the earth, both man and beast, creeping thing and birds of the air, for I am sorry that I have made them.' But Noah found grace in the eyes of the LORD."* NKJV

If you aren't careful, you might miss a couple of important facts in this "expression of grace." Read the verse that goes before the ones we have just read and then the one that follows them. Genesis 6:5 says: *"The LORD saw how great the wickedness of the human race had become on the earth, and that every inclination of the thoughts of the human heart was only evil all the time."* NIV Does that sound familiar to anyone? Now read the description of Noah given in the next verse: Genesis 6:9 *"Noah was a righteous man, blameless among the people of his time, and he walked faithfully with God."* NIV

Don't let anyone ever tell you that you can't live a righteous life in this day and age. If Noah could pull it off in the most corrupt culture of all time, we can certainly do it today!

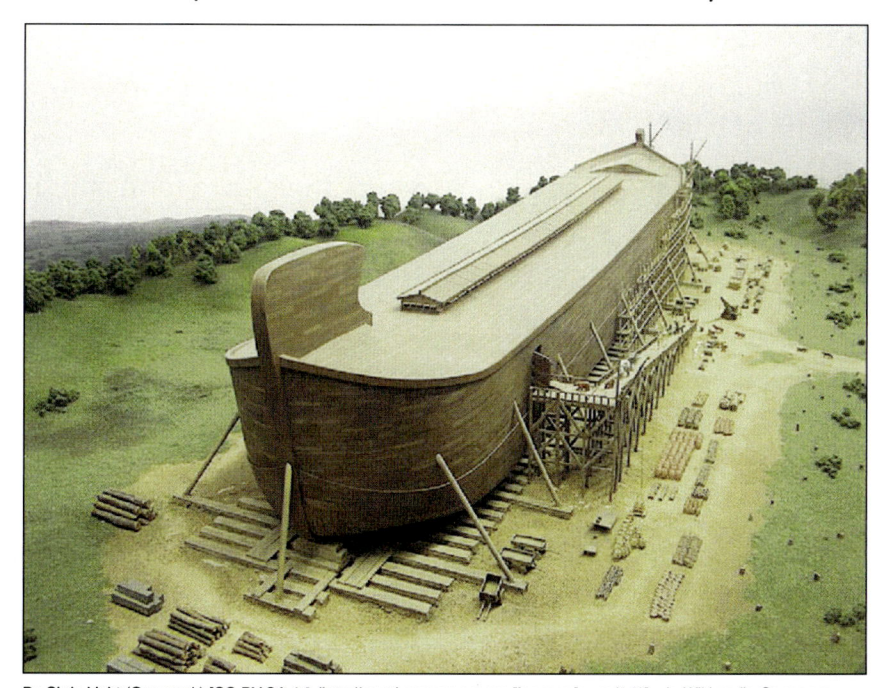

By Chris Light (Own work) [CC BY-SA 4.0 (http://creativecommons.org/licenses/by-sa/4.0)], via Wikimedia Commons

Teach Us To Pray | © 2019 | Prayerful Publishing Inc. | www.prayerfulpublishing.com | All Rights Reserved

Noah wasn't the only one who had a shot at God's grace. Noah spent 100 years building a 75 x 450 foot boat in a world that had never seen rain. It is entirely possible that those who watched him build that boat asked what he was doing and why he was doing it. Did they deserve to hear and see a message that invited them to repent? Nope, but God sent the message anyway. 2 Peter 2:5, 9 calls Noah a preacher of righteousness: *"if he did not spare the ancient world when he brought the flood on its ungodly people, but protected Noah, a preacher of righteousness, and seven others… then the Lord knows how to deliver the godly out of temptations and to reserve the unjust under punishment for the day of judgment."* NKJV

His actions… if not his very words… were a testimony to the entire world that judgment was coming. Apparently God did not find anyone else in Noah's generation who was willing to listen. Genesis 7:1 tells us: *"Then the Lord said to Noah, "Enter the ark, you and all your household, for you alone I have seen to be righteous before Me in this time."* NASB

The lesson from Noah's generation might be: **"When it come to God's grace… use it or lose it, but don't abuse it!"**

> *Review the following prayer prompts on grace. The prompts should help you in the "Did They Pursue Grace or did Grace Pursue Them?" exercise.*

When we come before God in prayer, we must understand that we are approaching the throne of grace. Grace, and grace alone, provides access and is the foundation for our requests.

Hebrews 4:16 *Therefore let us draw near with confidence to the throne of grace, so that we may receive mercy and find grace to help in time of need.* NASB

Grace is available for everyone, but only received by those who recognize their need for it and the source of supply.

Romans 3:23-24 *for all have sinned and fall short of the glory of God, being justified as a gift by His grace through the redemption which is in Christ Jesus* NASB

Acts 17:30-31 *"Therefore having overlooked the times of ignorance, God is now declaring to men that all people everywhere should repent, because He has fixed a day in which He will judge the world in righteousness through a Man whom He has appointed, having furnished proof to all men by raising Him from the dead."* NASB

While we cannot "earn" grace, there are some heart conditions that will restrict our access to God's grace. In fact, when we allow our hearts to be filled with pride, we may find resistance from God instead of grace.

1 Peter 5:5 *Likewise you younger people, submit yourselves to your elders. Yes, all of you be submissive to one another, and be clothed with humility, for "God resists the proud, but gives grace to the humble."* NLT

We don't earn grace by our good behavior. We accept it.

Ephesians 2:8-10 *God saved you by his grace when you believed. And you can't take credit for this; it is a gift from God. Salvation is not a reward for the good things we have done, so none of us can boast about it. For we are God's masterpiece. He has created us anew in Christ Jesus, so we can do the good things he planned for us long ago.* NLT

Many people view "grace" like the atmosphere. Once we walk into God's grace it surrounds us like the air we breathe. Perhaps we should think of it more like a garden that we have to grow. Perhaps we should prepare the soil, properly set the plants, keep the weeds out, water it regularly and always leave room for the plants to reach for the heavens.

2 Peter 3:18 *but grow in the grace and knowledge of our Lord and Savior Jesus Christ. To Him be the glory both now and forever. Amen.*

Romans 6:1-2 *What shall we say then? Shall we continue in sin that grace may abound? Certainly not! How shall we who died to sin live any longer in it?* NKJV

If you want to enter the royal court or the Oval office, you may need an introduction. Our access into the grace in which we stand is Jesus Christ our Redeemer.

Romans 5:2 *through whom also we have obtained our introduction by faith into this grace in which we stand; and we exult in hope of the glory of God.* NASB

God is not stingy with His grace. He is happy to give generously to those with the right attitude.

James 4:6 *And he gives grace generously. As the Scriptures say, "God opposes the proud, but gives grace to the humble."* NLT

God's nature of love and kindness is the driving force behind our standing with God. It is clearly His work in us, not our work for Him.

Titus 3:4-6 *But when the kindness of God our Savior and His love for mankind appeared, He saved us, not on the basis of deeds which we have done in righteousness, but according to His mercy, by the washing of regeneration and renewing by the Holy Spirit, whom He poured out upon us richly through Jesus Christ our Savior.* NASB

It is so easy to tell God that He has to be "fair with us"… that we deserve this or that. Our relationship with God begins with "undeserved grace" and continues with "undeserved grace". Let's make sure that we keep this truth in the front of our minds as we pray.

Acts 15:11 *We believe that we are all saved the same way, by the undeserved grace of the Lord Jesus.* NLT

Did They Pursue Grace or did Grace Pursue Them?

In each of these following examples you could make the case that both answers are true.
In spite of this fact, write down your best argument for one side or the other.

Adam & Eve – Genesis 3:6-19 Did grace pursue them, or did they pursue grace? _____

_____
_____
_____

Noah – Genesis 6:5-9 Did grace pursue him, or did he pursue grace? _____
_____
_____
_____

Abraham – Romans 4:1-8 Did grace pursue him, or did he pursue grace? _____
_____
_____
_____

Israelites in Egypt – Exodus 3:7-10 Did grace pursue them, or did they pursue grace? _____
_____
_____
_____

Rahab – Joshua 2:3-14 Did grace pursue her, or did she pursue grace? _____
_____
_____
_____

Jonah & Ninevites – Jonah 1:14; 2:2,10; 3:6-10; 4:2,11 Did grace pursue them, or did they pursue grace? _____
_____
_____

Hosea – Hosea 2:1-4, 14:1-9 Did grace pursue him, or did he pursue grace? _____
_____
_____
_____

Prodigal Son – Luke 15:11-14, 20-24 Did grace pursue him, or did he pursue grace? _____
_____
_____
_____

Thief on the cross – Luke 23:39-43 Did grace pursue him, or did he pursue grace? _____
_____
_____
_____

Peter after resurrection – Mark 14:27-31, 70-72; John 21:15-19 Did grace pursue him, or did he pursue grace? _____
_____
_____
_____

Paul on the road to Damascus – Acts 9:1-8, 13-16, 20 Did grace pursue him, or did he pursue grace? _____
_____
_____

How about you? – Did *grace pursue you?* If so, give a summary statement about the way "grace pursued you". _____
_____
_____
_____

How about you? – Did *you pursue grace?* If so, give a summary statement about how "you have pursued grace". _____
_____
_____
_____

We have been studying the Lord's Prayer for some time. Right now we are focused on how God desires to bring His kingdom into our lives. In Jesus' words: *"your kingdom come, your will be done on earth as it is in heaven."* **Grace is the only means of entry into God's heavenly kingdom.**

Our eternal existence will have grace at its very core. On earth, grace is meant to be the channel (life expression) of His Kingdom. Our Christian life (including our prayers) begins with embracing the grace of our Lord and finds expression through a grace-filled life.

- Notes -

Read Lesson 15 Short Story: HHU Vol. 2 - Searching For Paradise I

- Memory Verse -

For the grace of God that brings salvation has appeared to all men, teaching us that, denying ungodliness and worldly lusts, we should live soberly, righteously, and godly in the present age.

Titus 2:11-12 **NKJV**

Approach with Meekness

Lesson 16: Faith - Without this, pleasing God is impossible

Faith isn't a "hero or loser" concept.

Have you ever had a life changing experience? It's rare for most people… especially when we are young. For me, there were three that are forever etched into my memory. The first was being on the Sea of Galilee and imagining the faith that was needed to get out of the boat. We were floating along on a beautiful calm day, and I couldn't even imagine trying to walk on the water. Then I pictured a serious storm and my trepidation rose.

Photo by Author, The Garden Tomb, 2008

The second happened on the Temple Mount. There had been nearly 250,000 protesters who marched in an *intifada* that week. We entered the Temple Mount singing a worship chorus, and a Muslim sentry quickly told us that no singing or praying was allowed on the Temple Mount. Well, we didn't cross the ocean just to be told that we couldn't sing or pray in His Temple. I stood 75 feet away from the Muslim sentry, raised my hands to the Lord and silently prayed. Then, we walked across to the side that faced the Mount of Olives and sang worship choruses to the Lord. Foolishness or faith? Maybe a little of both, but we were not going to walk away from our chance to worship on the Temple Mount. The third, which will never be erased from our memories, was when we walked through the opening pictured above. It's called the Garden Tomb which sits adjacent to Skull Hill. As we walked through that opening, my wife and I, *"through the eyes of faith,"* envisioned the empty tomb that the women saw on that momentous morning.

There is a lot of confusion about "faith" in the Christian life. Clearly, it is a vital element of our Christian walk. **First, we must understand that God initiates the revelation of Himself to us.** If He didn't, we as finite man, could never comprehend the infinite God. We see the beginning of this in Romans 1:18-20 which says: *"For the wrath of God is revealed from heaven against all ungodliness and unrighteousness of men, who suppress the truth in unrighteousness, because what may be known of God is manifest in them, for God has shown it to them. For since the creation of the world His invisible attributes are clearly seen, being understood by the things that are made, even His eternal power and Godhead, so that they are without excuse."* NKJV

Every person who ever lived has this amazing revelation of God. He calls us to an even greater understanding, and some people are more responsive than others. According to Hebrews 11:6, God reveals Himself, which calls for a faith response. God says He will reward us for the right response. God also warns us against a failure to respond in faith as found in Matthew 11:21-24. That seems simple enough. In some ways it really is. In other ways, maybe not so much. The Bible has a lot to say on this subject, and we don't have enough time in one lesson to pursue every facet of this critical topic. So, we will simply take a look at the chapter known as the **faith hall of fame**. Hebrews 11 recounts what faith is (11:1), what is gained by faith (11:2,3,6), and lists examples of people who responded in faith (11:4-39).

Matching Exercise – Examples of Faith

1 ____ Wrestled with God to obtain a promised blessing

2 ____ Hid spies for Israel

3 ____ Proclaimed prophetic blessings to future generations on his deathbed

4 ____ Refused to become an Egyptian prince

5 ____ Appointed Saul to be the first king of Israel

6 ____ Made a better sacrifice to God than his brother

7 ____ Listened to a female prophetess and won a victory

8 ____ Gave a prophetic blessing on his twin boys

9 ____ Defeated an enormous army with 300 warriors

10 ____ Had a baby at age 90

11 ____ Defeated a 9' warrior with a sling

12 ____ First person to avoid physical death

13 ____ Set an enemy field on fire using foxes

14 ____ Probably spent 100 years on a faith building project

15 ____ Was 100 years old when his miracle child was born

A) Barak - Judges 4:14-15

B) Gideon - Judges 7:16-22

C) Enoch - Genesis 5:21-24

D) Isaac - Genesis 27:27-29, 38-40

E) Sarah - Genesis 17:15-17, 21:1-7

F) Rahab - Joshua 2:8-14

G) Samson - Judges 15:1-5

H) Joseph - Genesis 50:24-26

I) Jacob - Genesis 32:24-30

J) Samuel - 1 Samuel 8:3-6, 17-22

K) David - 1 Samuel 17:31-33, 46-50

L) Abel - Genesis 4:3-5

M) Moses - Exodus 2:10-15

N) Abraham - Genesis 21:5

O) Noah - Genesis 5:32, 7:6

Heroes Who Failed The Test

Some people might think that they can't be heroes of the faith like these men and women. We need to understand that they weren't perfect. Faith isn't a "hero or loser" concept, but a walking towards or walking away kind of thing. To realize this truth, we must look not only at the significant successes of these men and women, but also the fact that God understands our weaknesses.

Let's look at examples of people who at one point in their lives seemed to fail the test, but still made it to the "faith hall of fame." Write down how they might have failed to step forward in their faith.

Abraham – Genesis 12:10-14; 20:1-2, 10-13 _____

_____

Gideon – Judges 6:13-16, 36-40 _____

_____

Barak – Judges 4:5-9 _____

_____

Sarah – Genesis 16:1-4 _____

_____

Samson – Judges 16:15-20 _____

_____

Israel – 1 Samuel 8:1-8 _____

_____

David – 1 Samuel 21:1-2, 10-15 _____

_____

Moses – Exodus 4:1-5, 10-13 _____

_____

Teach Us To Pray I © 2019 I Prayerful Publishing Inc. I www.prayerfulpublishing.com I All Rights Reserved

Let's reflect upon New Testament leaders. Can you think of points in their lives where they seemed to fail to step forward in faith?

Peter – Matthew 14:15-32 _____

_____

Thomas and all the disciples the day after the crucifixion – Matt. 16:21-23, John 11:38-46, Mark 16:9-15 _____

_____

Church at Mary the mother of John's house – Acts 12:5, 12-15 _____

_____

What was Jesus' response to them, and what does that tell you to expect in His response to your steps of faith? _____

_____

What does that tell you personally about stepping out in faith in order to follow Jesus? _____

_____

_____

Let's close today's lesson by acknowledging that none of us will have perfect faith. Like a baby learning to walk, we must take that first step. We must learn to walk before we can run. Ultimately, we must move on to "walk by faith" (2 Corinthians 5:7), and then "run the race set before us" by following the examples of men and women of faith (Hebrews 12:1). God accepts our imperfect steps of faith as evidenced by Jesus' response to the man in Mark 9:24 who said he believed… and followed that with "help me with my unbelief." He challenged Thomas to examine the evidence of His nail-scarred hands and feet, but He didn't reject him. Jesus invited Peter to walk on the water, then reached out His hand to pull him up when he started to sink. He will do the same for each of us. Like any loving parent, God will pick us up when we fall, put His arms around us, and help us get our balance so we can move on to the next level in our faith walk.

Read Lesson 16 Short Story: HHU Vol. 1 - God's Provision

– Memory Verse –

But without faith it is impossible to please Him, for he who comes to God must believe that He is, and that He is a rewarder of those who diligently seek Him.
Hebrews 11:6 **NKJV**

Approach with Meekness

Lesson 17: Joy - You'll find it here!

In His presence is fullness of joy!

"I knew this would happen. Now everything is ruined! I have dreamt of this day since I was a little girl. I planned every detail to perfection, and now it's over. My dream day just went down the drain!" "I understand, but I told you that almost every wedding has a hiccup." "A hiccup? A hiccup?? The flowers are ruined... our hair and makeup is trashed... not to mention what the wedding photos will look like! How could it rain on my wedding day?" "Trust me... years from now you won't be talking about those things. You'll be focusing on how beautiful or smart your children are, or about how challenging your work is. The important thing is, you are marrying a great guy who loves you a lot." "Why are you treating this like it's no big deal? It's a big deal to me!" "I want you to believe me about this. When you look back on this day, you won't look for joy in the flowers, the music, the dresses or the pictures. You will look for the joy in his eyes." "You are such a guy. You just don't get it!"

That fictional conversation serves as an illustration of the fact that things can go wrong... sometimes very wrong... with weddings, and just about anything else in life. **Life is just like that.** The person who comes with the expectation that *everything is going to be perfect and nothing can or ever will go wrong* is going to be disappointed.

Does that mean that we should walk through our lives expecting to live with disappointment? Jesus set much higher expectations. He said: *"My purpose is to give them a rich and satisfying life."* John 10:10b NLT Jesus was very clear about what His intent is for our lives. In the same verse, He was also clear about the intent our spiritual enemy has for our lives: *"The thief's purpose is to steal and kill and destroy."* John 10:10a NLT If we apply that indiscriminately to our daily lives (like in the wedding illustration), we can easily get confused. Did God or Satan bring rain on their wedding day? We don't know for sure. God is sovereign in our lives, but Satan is always trying to destroy things. My advice to the bride would be: "Don't let Satan steal your joy. This is designed to be one of the best days of your life. Prepare as well as you possibly can. Allow for contingencies, but always keep your eyes on the prize." My advice to the groom would be pretty similar: "Do everything you can to make your bride happy on this day. This day is all about the start of a fulfilling relationship with that young woman."

OK, the illustration went on a little long. Please indulge the author at this point. Weeks before writing this lesson, I had the privilege of officiating my son's wedding. The point may be long, but it is valid. If we are going to enjoy the abundant life that God desires for us, we will have to keep our eyes on the prize. What is that prize? It is a vibrant relationship with the living God. There are a lot of challenges and distractions that Satan will provide along the way.

Let's look together at a good example of this from Luke 15. In this example the roles of the shepherd, woman and two sons represent our pursuit of a relationship with God.

What possible challenges or distractions might prevent the restoration of their relationship with God? What was the result when the situation was resolved?

What were some of the challenges or distractions the *shepherd* might have faced? _____
_____

What was the result when the situation was resolved? _____
_____

What were some of the challenges or distractions the *woman* might have faced? _____
_____

What was the result when the situation was resolved? _____
_____

What were some of the challenges or distractions the *younger brother* might have faced? _____
_____

What was the result when the situation was resolved? _____
_____

What were some of the challenges or distractions the *older brother* might have faced? _____
_____

What was the result when the situation was resolved? _____
_____

Which of those challenges or distractions *would you* find most difficult to overcome? _____
_____

What will be the result when your situation is resolved? _____
_____

Searching for Joy Exercise

In the following exercise, fill in the blank spaces in order to complete the sentences. Be sure to utilize the correct version of the Bible. When they are complete, place the Scripture reference in one of the three columns in the *Where Joy Comes From* table.

Isaiah 12:2-3 NASB Behold, God is my _____, I will _____ and not be _____; For the LORD GOD is my _____ and _____, And He has become my _____. Therefore you will _____ draw _____ from the _____ of salvation.

Nehemiah 12:43 NLT Many sacrifices were offered on that _____ day, for God had given the people cause for _____ _____. The women and children also _____ in the _____, and the _____ of the people of Jerusalem could be heard far away.

Galatians 5:22-23 NLT But the _____ _____ produces this kind of _____ in our lives: love, _____, peace, _____, kindness, goodness, faithfulness, _____, and self-control. There is no law against these things!

Romans 15:13 NASB Now may the God of hope fill you with all _____ and _____ in believing, so that you will abound in _____ by the _____ of the Holy Spirit.

Jeremiah 31:12 NLT They will come home and sing _____ of _____ on the heights of Jerusalem. They will be _____ because of the LORD's good _____ — the _____ crops of grain, new wine, and olive oil, and the _____ flocks and herds. Their _____ will be like a watered garden, and all their _____ will be gone.

Psalm 4:7 NLT You have given me _____ _____ than those who have _____ harvests of _____ and new _____.

Philippians 1:4 NASB Always offering _____ with _____ in my every _____ for you all.

Isaiah 56:7 NASB Even those I will bring to My holy mountain And make them _____ in My house of _____. Their burnt offerings and their sacrifices will be _____ on My altar; For My house will be called a house of _____ for all the peoples.

Teach Us To Pray I © 2019 I Prayerful Publishing Inc. I www.prayerfulpublishing.com I All Rights Reserved

29

Acts 13:52 NKJV And the disciples were _____ with _____ and with the _____ _____.

Luke 1:46-49 NKJV And Mary said: "My soul _____ the Lord, and my spirit has _____ in God my Savior. For He has regarded the lowly state of His maidservant; for behold, henceforth all generations will call me _____. For He who is mighty has done _____ _____ for me, and holy is His name."

Psalm 28:7 NIV The Lord is my _____ and my _____; my heart _____ in him, and he _____ me. My _____ leaps for _____, and with my song I _____ him.

Philippians 3:1 NLT _____ happens, my dear brothers and sisters, _____ in the Lord. I never get tired of telling you these things, and I do it to _____ your faith.

Luke 24:52-53 NLT They _____ him and then returned to Jerusalem _____ with _____ _____. And they spent all of their time in the Temple, _____ God.

Psalm 16:11 NASB You will make known to me the _____ of life; In Your _____ is _____ of _____; In Your _____ hand there are _____ forever.

2 Chronicles 6:41 NASB Now therefore arise, O LORD God, to Your resting place, You and the ark of Your might; let Your priests, O LORD God, be clothed with _____ and let Your godly ones _____ in what is _____.

Philippians 4:4 NLT _____ be _____ of _____ in the Lord. I say it again – _____!

Psalm 21:6 NIV Surely you have granted him _____ _____ and made him _____ with the _____ of your _____.

Psalm 43:4 NLT There I will go to the altar of God, to God – the _____ of all my _____. I will _____ you with my harp, O God, my God!

Philippians 2:18 NASB You too, I urge you, _____ in the same way and _____ your _____ with me.

Isaiah 9:3 NKJV You have multiplied the nation and _____ its _____; They _____ before You according to the _____ of _____, as men rejoice when they divide the _____.

Where Joy Comes From Exercise

In the following exercise, reflect on the Scriptures from the **Searching For Joy Exercise**, and place each verse in one of the three categories listed in the table below. For example, would Isaiah 12:2-3 be an expression of Joy *as a gift*, Joy *as a choice*, or Joy *in response to God's goodness*. In most of the Scriptures you may be able to make a case for any of the categories. Select the category that is the best choice from your point of view.

Joy is a gift	Joy is a choice	Joy is a response to God's goodness

Read Lesson 17 Short Story: HHU Vol. 2 - A Closer Walk

- Memory Verse -

I am overwhelmed with joy in the LORD my God! For he has dressed me with the clothing of salvation and draped me in a robe of righteousness. I am like a bridegroom in his wedding suit or a bride with her jewels. Isaiah 61:10 **NLT**

Approach with Devotion

Lesson 18: Fellowship - Our souls long for intimacy

> *Fellowship is the sweetness of one soul truly connecting with another.*

"There is something terribly wrong with this!" "What are you talking about?" "We came up here to enjoy the great outdoors… to reconnect with one another… to get away from our everyday life. And here we are sitting around a campfire with everyone staring at their cell phones. I didn't even think we could get coverage way up here." "Dad, you don't understand. I was just texting God to tell Him how beautiful everything is up here." "That's just stupid, Sis… everyone knows that God uses Twitter now." "Would you guys just quit your bickering and put another log on the fire!"

Of course, in that fictitious camping scene, both of the siblings are technically incorrect. God doesn't use either texts or Twitter. Jeremiah 17:10 tells us: *"I the LORD search the heart and examine the mind, to reward each person according to their conduct, according to what their deeds deserve."* NIV If that is true, and God's Word is never wrong, then God knows what we think and feel about something without getting a text message. So why are we even talking about "prayer"? What's in it for God? What's in it for us? The answer may be found by answering this question.

Why did our fictitious family go camping? Why would your family go camping? Don't we already know one another pretty well? Many of our families spend a lot of time together. I know this… when my wife and I get home from work, we don't text or tweet one another about our day. We talk. Why? We talk because we care. We want to see the expression on their face… hear the tone of their voice and even watch their body language as they walk through the door. We are in a close relationship, and unlike God, we won't know the thoughts and intents of their hearts without listening.

There is another reason. That would be so that the other person has a chance to tell their story. Sometimes we need the privilege of sharing the excitement of our really good news. There are times that we need to "vent" about something. We need the chance to get it out… we need to be heard. God knows that. Search the Scriptures and you will find God asking people questions when He already knew the answer. *Adam… where are you?* (Genesis 3:9) *What is the matter with you, Hagar?* (Genesis 21:17) *What are you doing here Elijah?* (1 Kings 19:9,13) *Woman, why are you weeping? Whom are you seeking?* (John 20:15) *Saul, Saul, why are you persecuting Me?* (Acts 9:4) The questions weren't about God needing to discover the answer. Those questions were designed to help the person discover something. Something they needed to learn through speaking (voicing) their answer out loud.

Picture this! Your parents know that you got an A on a test. Imagine them asking how you did, simply so that you would have the joy of telling your story. How would that bring you closer in your relationship with them? Let's say your parent knows that you did something wrong or dishonest. Can you picture them asking you about it with the goal of letting you reveal the truth? How could that create distance in... or possibly enhance... your relationship?

It is one thing to be asked about things that the other person already knows. It is quite another thing to share secrets with a trusted friend. Imagine yourself taking a road trip with your best friend. The only purpose of the trip is found in sharing extended and unguarded conversations. If you've never been on a trip like that, you are truly missing out. That day will certainly come and you will file it in your bank of treasured memories.

There is something very special about time spent sitting around a campfire with the ones we love and reflecting on a day spent walking through the trees, or viewing a majestic vista. There is something special about a long conversation with a trusted friend... talking about things that only a friend would truly understand. For some settings that might be called intimacy. For other settings it might be called having a best friend. In the Christian world we use the word "**fellowship**." It is the sweetness of one soul truly connecting with another. That is what God desires in our relationship with Him. When our souls have found that sweet connection with God, what naturally follows is a genuine connection with the rest of His children. This is greatly enhanced when we share our intimate concerns as we pray with and for one another.

There are some things that enhance our fellowship with God and His children, and things which detract from that fellowship. Look up the Scripture verses found in the middle column. In the table below write a word or phrase to describe what will enhance or detract from our fellowship. In most cases you will find answers that will only fit in the Enhance or Detract column. Some of the verses will allow for answers in both columns.

Key Word/Phrase that ENHANCES FELLOWSHIP	Scripture Verses	Key Word/Phrase that DETRACTS FELLOWSHIP
	1 John 1:3	
	Acts 2:42	
	Philemon 1:6	
	John 12:35	
	2 Corinthians 6:14	
	Philippians 1:4-5	
	1 John 1:6	
	Ephesians 5:11	
	Philippians 3:10-11	
	John 17:3, 21	
	Colossians 3:14	
	Ephesians 4:13	
	1 Corinthians 1:9-10	
	Philippians 2:1-3	
	1 John 1:7	
	Galatians 2:9	
	Romans 6:5	
	Ephesians 4:3	
	Philippians 1:7-9	
	Colossians 1:9-12	
	John 8:12	

Review the homework short story, "**Details**." What kinds of things helped enhance or detracted from the relationships of the characters? How would praying with others provide a similar role in enhancing or detracting from our relational connections?

_____ What was the sport that Hank and Gary played that helped them develop a closer relationship?
    A. tennis   **B.** basketball   **C.** softball   **D.** soccer

How do you think that might have helped them connect relationally? _____
_____
How might praying with others provide a similar relational connection for people? _____
_____

_____ How often did Hank and Gary meet at the coffee shop?
    A. once a week **B.** once a month **C.** 4 or 5 times a week **D.** 4 or 5 times a year

How do you think that might have helped them connect relationally? _____
_____
How might praying with others provide a similar relational connection for people? _____
_____

_____ What prompted Hank to make the commitment to meet with Gary?
    A. the death of Gary's wife/Hank's sister   **B.** business investment advice
    C. fans of the same football team   **D.** loved working on old cars

How do you think that might have helped them connect relationally? _____
_____
How might praying with others provide a similar relational connection for people? _____
_____

_____ What provided a distraction to Hank and Gary's close relationship?
    A. their children **B.** no time because of work schedules **C.** financial success
    D. strong opinions about politics

How do you think that might have harmed their ability to connect relationally? _____
_____
How might avoiding prayer create a similar relational problem for people? _____
_____

_____ What prompted Gahiji to stop and ask Hank to pray with him?

    A. they were friends from high school   **B.** Gahiji thought Hank was a pastor

    C. they were from the same church   **D.** violent threats in a foreign land

How do you think that might have helped them connect relationally? _____

_____

How might praying with others provide a similar relational connection for people? _____

_____

_____ Why did Hank hesitate to invite Gahiji into his house?

    A. he was afraid that his dog would bite him   **B.** Gahiji's shoes were muddy

    C. he thought Gahiji would be asking him for money   **D.** Hank was a racist

How do you think that inviting him in might have helped them connect relationally? _____

_____

How might praying with others provide a similar relational connection for people? _____

_____

- Notes -

_____

_____

_____

Read Lesson 18 Short Story: HHU Vol. 2 - Details

- Memory Verse -

I thank my God upon every remembrance of you, always in every prayer of mine making request for you all with joy.

Philippians 1:3-4 **NKJV**

Approach with Devotion

Lesson 19: Submission - Let's talk about this

> **Deo Volente**
> *Your will be done on earth as it is in heaven.*

"I hate Thanksgiving!" "What's your problem with Thanksgiving? It's my favorite holiday. What's not to like? Turkey… dressing… pumpkin pie… family… what's not to like?" "You just answered your own question. It's not so great when you are not with family on Thanksgiving." "I'm so sorry, man. I forgot that you left home a couple years ago. Why did you leave, anyway?" "I needed a *life*, and it wasn't going to happen in that house." "I heard that your father came by your work. I think you might have been off that day. He told one of the guys that he really missed you." "Yah, Yah. I heard about that. He wrote me a letter saying he always loved me and was crushed when I left." "So, what happened after that?" "Nothing happened after that. I've watched my friends with their fathers. Their dads have rules they want them to follow. Forget that! He actually invited me up to the family cabin. I figured it couldn't hurt. Right? It was all… everybody be cool with your brother. They tried really hard to be extra nice to me, but I knew it wasn't real. In the end I knew they all had expectations. Dads especially seem to have 'house rules' if you know what I mean? He expects me to respect him and the rest of the family. I like being independent, so I walked away. Hey, at least I have a shot at the inheritance." "So, you just walked away and never went back?" "Yep… that's right. They invite me to join them every Thanksgiving and Christmas, but I say… sorry… not interested!" "But I thought you said you were bummed about Thanksgiving because you didn't have any family? So, you want the inheritance, but none of the hassles, is that it?" "You got it!"

http://www.lakegeorgeescape.com/wp-content/uploads/2012/06/Campfire-teens.jpg

Heaven will be a great family reunion… a time of Thanksgiving if you will. Hell will be knowing that you chose to walk away.

There is only one place in the universe where rebellion can exist long term. It's not in heaven. It exists (usually unsuccessfully) on this planet for a limited amount of time. It either gets crushed… or wins out… and then the rebellion crushes those who resist its newfound authority.

Do you believe that people will get away with shaking their fists in defiance of God in heaven? Do you believe that people will be able to get away with deceit about their rebellion in heaven? The Lord's prayer teaches us to pray: *"Your will be done on earth as it is in heaven."*

Can we really pray that without recognizing that it is God's desire that we take delight in doing His will "**right here and now**"?

Let's start by taking a look at what we *will find* and *will not find* in heaven. As part of this exercise, you should also look for *the traits* of those who will or will not inherit eternal life. In some of these verses, heaven may not be directly referenced, but would implied by the context. This exercise will help us understand what *"Your will be done on earth as it is in heaven"* might really mean.

Found or Not Found in Heaven Exercise

According to Jesus' own words	This will be in heaven Traits of those in heaven	This will not be in heaven Traits of those not in heaven
Matthew 5:12		
Matthew 7:13-14		
Matthew 8:11-12		
John 14:2-3		
Matthew 10:32-33		
Luke 23:42-43		
Matthew 13:40-43		
Matthew 18:3-4		
Matthew 18:10		
Matthew 22:29-32		
Matthew 23:29, 33		
Luke 13:24, 27-29		
Matthew 25:30		
John 5:24-29		
Matthew 25:41-46		

According to the Apostles, Luke and Author of Hebrews	This will be in heaven Traits of those in heaven	This will not be in heaven Traits of those not in heaven
Acts 17:30-31		
Romans 1:18-20		
Romans 2:4-10		
1 Corinthians 6:9-11		
Galatians 5:19-21		
Ephesians 1:18-22		
Ephesians 2:3-7		
Ephesians 5:5-7		
Philippians 3:19-21		
Colossians 3:1-6		
2 Thessalonians 1:6-9		
Hebrews 1:2-3, 8:1, 12:2		
1 Peter 1:3-5		
2 Peter 2:4,9		
2 Peter 3:13		

- Notes -

According to the Apostle John	This will be in heaven Traits of those in heaven	This will not be in heaven Traits of those not in heaven
John 3:15-18		
John 3:36		
1 John 2:16-17		
Revelation 7:11		
Revelation 7:13-14		
Revelation 7:16		
Revelation 7:17		
Revelation 20:10-14		
Revelation 20:15		
Revelation 21:4		
Revelation 21:8		
Revelation 21:22-27		
Revelation 22:2		
Revelation 22:3		
Revelation 22:5		

Reflect on the traits of those who will live in heaven, then write a brief summary of what doing God's will might look like there.

_____
_____
_____
_____
_____

Your will be done on earth as it is in heaven.

In our next lesson we will take a more comprehensive look at God's will. In today's lesson we will look at one particular facet of His will. One of the expressed desires of God's will for us here on earth is to submit to those to whom God has given responsibility and authority.

In this exercise, review the following Scripture verses, and then circle the God-ordained person or agency referenced in that passage. A case could be made for multiple choices for each passage. Select the one that you believe is the very best fit. All of these verses will be from the New King James Bible.

God-ordained Authority Exercise

Colossians 1:16-17 For by Him all things were created that are in heaven and that are on earth, visible and invisible, whether thrones or dominions or principalities or powers. All things were created through Him and for Him. And He is before all things, and in Him all things consist.

JESUS   GOVERNMENT   PASTOR/ELDER   ONE ANOTHER   PARENTS   SPOUSE

Romans 13:1-2 Let every soul be subject to the governing authorities. For there is no authority except from God, and the authorities that exist are appointed by God. Therefore whoever resists the authority resists the ordinance of God, and those who resist will bring judgment on themselves.

JESUS   GOVERNMENT   PASTOR/ELDER   ONE ANOTHER   PARENTS   SPOUSE

Ephesians 1:20-22 ...which He worked in Christ when He raised Him from the dead and seated *Him* at His right hand in the heavenly *places*, far above all principality and power and might and dominion, and every name that is named, not only in this age but also in that which is to come. And He put all *things* under His feet, and gave Him *to be* head over all *things* to the church.

JESUS   GOVERNMENT   PASTOR/ELDER   ONE ANOTHER   PARENTS   SPOUSE

Colossians 3:20 Children, obey your parents in all things, for this is well pleasing to the Lord.

JESUS   GOVERNMENT   PASTOR/ELDER   ONE ANOTHER   PARENTS   SPOUSE

Hebrews 13:17 Obey those who rule over you, and be submissive, for they watch out for your souls, as those who must give account. Let them do so with joy and not with grief, for that would be unprofitable for you.

JESUS   GOVERNMENT   PASTOR/ELDER   ONE ANOTHER   PARENTS   SPOUSE

Titus 2:9 Exhort bondservants to be obedient to their own masters, to be well pleasing in all *things*, not answering back.

JESUS   GOVERNMENT   PASTOR/ELDER   ONE ANOTHER   PARENTS   SPOUSE

Philippians 2:10-11 That at the name of Jesus every knee should bow, of those in heaven, and of those on earth, and of those under the earth, and *that* every tongue should confess that Jesus Christ *is* Lord, to the glory of God the Father.

JESUS   GOVERNMENT   PASTOR/ELDER   ONE ANOTHER   PARENTS   SPOUSE

Ephesians 5:22 Wives, submit yourselves to your own husbands as you do to the Lord.

JESUS   GOVERNMENT   PASTOR/ELDER   ONE ANOTHER   PARENTS   SPOUSE

John 17:2 ...as You have given Him authority over all flesh, that He should give eternal life to as many as You have given Him. as You have given Him authority over all flesh, that He should give eternal life to as many as You have given Him.

JESUS   GOVERNMENT   PASTOR/ELDER   ONE ANOTHER   PARENTS   SPOUSE

1 Peter 5:5 Likewise you younger people, submit yourselves to your elders. Yes, all of *you* be submissive to one another, and be clothed with humility, for "God resists the proud, but gives grace to the humble."

JESUS   GOVERNMENT   PASTOR/ELDER   ONE ANOTHER   PARENTS   SPOUSE

Colossians 4:1 Masters, give your bondservants what is just and fair, knowing that you also have a Master in heaven.

JESUS   GOVERNMENT   PASTOR/ELDER   ONE ANOTHER   PARENTS   SPOUSE

1 Corinthians 16:15-16 I urge you, brethren – you know the household of Stephanas, that it is the firstfruits of Achaia, and that *they* have devoted themselves to the ministry of the saints – that you also submit to such, and to everyone who works and labors with *us*.

JESUS   GOVERNMENT   PASTOR/ELDER   ONE ANOTHER   PARENTS   SPOUSE

Ephesians 6:1 Children, obey your parents in the Lord, for this is right.

JESUS   GOVERNMENT   PASTOR/ELDER   ONE ANOTHER   PARENTS   SPOUSE

Matthew 28:18 And Jesus came and spoke to them, saying, "All authority has been given to Me in heaven and on earth."

JESUS   GOVERNMENT   PASTOR/ELDER   ONE ANOTHER   PARENTS   SPOUSE

Ephesians 5:21 ...submitting to one another in the fear of God.

JESUS   GOVERNMENT   PASTOR/ELDER   ONE ANOTHER   PARENTS   SPOUSE

1 Thessalonians 5:12-13 And we urge you, brethren, to recognize those who labor among you, and are over you in the Lord and admonish you, and to esteem them very highly in love for their work's sake. Be at peace among yourselves.

JESUS   GOVERNMENT   PASTOR/ELDER   ONE ANOTHER   PARENTS   SPOUSE

Colossians 3:22-23 Bondservants, obey in all things your masters according to the flesh, not with eyeservice, as men-pleasers, but in sincerity of heart, fearing God. And whatever you do, do it heartily, as to the Lord and not to men.

JESUS   GOVERNMENT   PASTOR/ELDER   ONE ANOTHER   PARENTS   SPOUSE

Titus 3:1 Remind them to be subject to rulers and authorities, to obey, to be ready for every good work.

JESUS   GOVERNMENT   PASTOR/ELDER   ONE ANOTHER   PARENTS   SPOUSE

Colossians 3:24 knowing that from the Lord you will receive the reward of the inheritance; for you serve the Lord Christ.

JESUS   GOVERNMENT   PASTOR/ELDER   ONE ANOTHER   PARENTS   SPOUSE

Philippians 2:12-13 Therefore, my beloved, as you have always obeyed, not as in my presence only, but now much more in my absence, work out your own salvation with fear and trembling.

JESUS   GOVERNMENT   PASTOR/ELDER   ONE ANOTHER   PARENTS   SPOUSE

Write down what doing God's will on earth as it is in heaven might look like for you. _____

_____

_____

Read Lesson 19 Short Story: HHU Vol. 1 - It Is Finished

- Memory Verse -

"Go and make disciples of all nations, baptizing them in the name of the Father and of the Son and of the Holy Spirit, and teaching them to obey everything I have commanded you. And surely I am with you always, to the very end of the age."   Matthew 28:19-20 **NIV**

Approach with Devotion

Lesson 20: Abiding - It's a matter of life and death.

> **FYI:** *God is not on your beck and call list!*

"Wow! Is your mom ever ticked at you!" "What are you talking about?" "I'm not sure what you did, but I could see it on her face. You are in trouble… big trouble!" "Don't worry about it. She'll get over it. She always does." "So… whatever it is… you are just going to sweep it under the rug and wait for things to blow over?" "Yep. Works every time. She calms down and before you know it, everything is fine." "So… you and your Mom are really close? Is that right?" "I wouldn't say that, but we're still talking to one another."

Some people treat their connection with God like it is a "I'll get back to you if and when it works out best for me" situation. FYI: *God is not on your beck and call list.*

There are all kinds of ways to respond to people when they call us on our cell phone. If you have the identify feature, you could decide that you are too busy and you will call back later… or maybe you won't. You might decide that the person who is calling is so important that you will break away from your present conversation and take that call right away… or maybe not. If you see a text message you can respond at your leisure.

When it's God calling, a wise person will take that call and/or message. Why is it some choose to think this might be a take it or leave it conversation?

We have already looked at the *"Your will be done on earth as it is in heaven"* element of the Lord's prayer. We might need to ask ourselves if we really mean that. God has made His will clear about a lot of things. We are going to look at some of them in the coming exercise.

The first and most critical issue would be: Have I totally yielded to the concept of doing what God asks me to do? John 12:24-26 NLT puts it this way: *"I tell you the truth, unless a kernel of wheat is planted in the soil and dies, it remains alone. But its death will produce many new kernels—a plentiful harvest of new lives. Those who love their life in this world will lose it. Those who care nothing for their life in this world will keep it for eternity. Anyone who wants to serve me must follow me, because my servants must be where I am. And the Father will honor anyone who serves me."*

We have already discussed how Lucifer's desire to be in control created a rift in the heavenlies. For some reason it is easy for us to assume that we can choose our own path of obedience or disobedience. Jesus brought real clarity in the passage we have just looked at. We have to put the idea of pursuing our own agenda/path/directions in the ground. That has to die before we can be fruitful and reap a harvest.

Until that issue is resolved, we can accomplish nothing. John 15:4-5 NKJV says: *"Abide in Me, and I in you. As the branch cannot bear fruit of itself, unless it abides in the vine, neither can you, unless you abide in Me. "I am the vine, you are the branches. He who abides in Me, and I in him, bears much fruit; for without Me you can do nothing."*

The most natural thing to do is to pursue a "selfish motivation" in life. Jesus calls us to flip that upside down and through His strength and power, pursue a "God centered and others centered" motivation. That's not the way we are naturally wired. That kind of life requires a true transformation. God's power and His love (i.e. His Spirit in us) can make this possible. His love produces a supernatural flow of power in our lives. It looks like this… Jesus creates a wellspring of love flowing out of our lives.

We talked about following God's will in our lives in our last session. We have to understand that it isn't a matter of trying harder to obey God through our determined effort. **It is a matter of the wellspring of Jesus' love being expressed in obedience through us.**

Once we embrace this new paradigm, we will find that pursuing God's will is not an obligation. It is a supernatural cause and effect of abiding in Christ. The natural and supernatural effect of a rose bud would be the beautiful aroma produced by the rose plant. The observation of those who stop to smell the roses would be the pleasing aroma and beauty of a rose in full bloom. All the rose blossom had to do to create this effect would be to stay connected to the branch.

In like manner, when we stay connected to the love of Christ, the natural outflow would be obedience to the will of God which creates the aroma of Christ. 2 Corinthians 2:14-16 TLB says it this way: *But thanks be to God! For through what Christ has done, he has triumphed over us so that now wherever we go he uses us to tell others about the Lord and to spread the Gospel like a sweet perfume.*

As far as God is concerned there is a sweet, wholesome fragrance in our lives. It is the fragrance of Christ within us, an aroma to both the saved and the unsaved all around us. To those who are not being saved, we seem a fearful smell of death and doom, while to those who know Christ we are a life-giving perfume.

> *"If you abide in Me, and My words abide in you, you will ask what you desire, and it shall be done for you."*

Once that issue is fully resolved, God can easily answer our prayers and honor our efforts. John 15:7 NKJV says: *"If you abide in Me, and My words abide in you, you will ask what you desire, and it shall be done for you."* Let's take a look at what that might mean by reviewing some of the elements of "Your will be done on earth, as it is in heaven."

It's God's work… not our work… **it's God's life in us**. Let's take a look at how pursuing God's will by staying connected to the branch is as simple as **A - B - C**.

God's Will is as easy as A-B-C

Review the Scriptures listed in the right columns, and in the left tab/column rank the clarity of God's will using the following measures. Rank them using numbers 1, 2 or 3.

1 - This is a clear and direct expression of God's will for every human being.

2 - This calls for a specific plan, behavior or activity that God wants in each of our lives.

3 - This represents a principle that all Christians should live by in their daily lives.

The verses are summarized for the sake of brevity. You can look them up to get the exact wording and/or full context.

	A - Exodus 20:2-3 I am the Lord your God. You shall have no other Gods before Me.
	B - 2 Peter 3:9 It is not God's will that any should perish, but that all should come to repentance.
	C - 1 Thessalonians 4:3 It is God's will that you be sanctified and abstain from sexual immorality.
	D - Luke 10:27 Love the Lord your God with all your heart and with all your soul and with all your strength and with all your mind; and love your neighbor as yourself.
	E - Exodus 20:13 You shall not murder.
	F - John 6:40 God desires that everyone sees the Son and believes in Him.
	G - 1 Thessalonians 5:18 In everything give thanks.
	H - Proverbs 3:5 Trust in the Lord with all your heart and don't lean on your own understanding.
	I - Exodus 20:7 Don't take the name of the Lord in vain.
	J - Matthew 28:19 Go into all the world and preach the gospel.
	K - Romans 12:2 Be transformed by the renewing of your mind so that you may prove that the will of God is good and acceptable and perfect.
	L - Acts 2:38 Repent and be baptized for the forgiveness of your sins and you will receive the gift of the Holy Spirit.
	M - 1 Peter 2:15 It is God's will that by doing good you should silence foolish people.
	N - Exodus 20:12 Honor your father and mother.
	O - Luke 9:23 Whoever wants to be my disciple must deny himself, take up his cross and follow me.
	P - Matthew 22:39 You shall love your neighbor as yourself.
	Q - 1 Thessalonians 5:17 Pray without ceasing.
	R - 1 Timothy 2:3-4 God desires that all people be saved and come to the knowledge of the truth.
	S - Exodus 20:14 Don't commit adultery.

T -	Ephesians 5:17-18 Do not get drunk with wine, but be filled with the Holy Spirit.
U -	Micah 6:8 And what does the Lord require of you? To act justly and to love mercy and to walk humbly with your God.
V -	Ephesians 6:1-2 Children, obey your parents in the Lord, for this is right. "Honor your father and mother," which is the first commandment with promise.
W -	Exodus 20:15 You shall not steal.
X -	1 Peter 1:15-16 You shall be holy, for I am holy.
Y -	Matthew 5:48 You shall be perfect, as your Father in Heaven in perfect.
Z -	John 13:34 You shall love one another as I have loved you.

You might feel like the last three (and maybe more of these directives) are impossible. You would be right. You can't do it on your own. God's will being done on earth as it is in heaven is impossible. Jesus made this clear in Matthew 19:26 NLT where it says: Jesus looked at them intently and said, *"Humanly speaking, it is impossible, but with God everything is possible."* How does this happen you might ask?

John 14:16-17 NLT tells us: *And I will ask the Father, and he will give you another Advocate, who will never leave you. He is the Holy Spirit, who leads into all truth. The world cannot receive him, because it isn't looking for him and doesn't recognize him. But you know him, because he lives with you now and later will be in you.* In other words, God is going to live inside you and that will make doing His will possible.

How much does a branch have to do to grow and produce fruit? The branch has to stay attached to the vine (i.e. abide). The vine has to sink its roots deep into good soil. The branches reach up for the sunlight (i.e. do the very thing they are designed to do). God takes care of the rest. He sends the rain and the sunshine. He tends the soil so that it has the nutrients the vine needs in order to flourish. Is your heart attached to the vine (Jesus) and reaching for the sunlight (the Spirit of God)? Don't try to create the flow, go with the flow. At the very least, do your best to avoid hindering the flow. The Father is the vinedresser. He's going to take care of you. God's got it from here… relax. Quit striving and know that He is God (Psalm 46:10). ***God's will is not a list… it's a life. It is His life flowing through you!***

Read the following verses from the Prayer Prompts homework and fill in the blanks to discover the likely outcomes for a person who is abiding in Christ.

John 15:5 NKJV "I am the vine, you are the branches; he who abides in Me and I in him, he _____ much _____, for apart from Me you can do _____."

1 John 5:12 NKJV He who has the Son has _____; he who does not have the Son of God does not have _____.

John 15:7 NKJV If you abide in Me, and My words abide in you, you will _____ what you _____, and it shall be _____ for you.

John 8:47; 10:27 NKJV "He who is of God _____ God's words; therefore you do not hear, because you are not of God." My sheep _____ My _____, and I _____ them, and they _____ Me.

John 15:7-8 NKJV "If you abide in Me, and My words abide in you. This is to my Father's _____, that you _____ much _____, showing yourselves to be my _____."

Write a brief summary of the outcomes that will flow from a life that abides in Christ. _____

- Notes -

Read Lesson 20 Short Story: HHU Vol. 2 - Crisis

- Memory Verse -

"If you remain in me and my words remain in you, ask whatever you wish, and it will be given you. This is to my Father's glory, that you bear much fruit, showing yourselves to be my disciples. As the Father has loved me, so have I loved you. Now remain in my love."
John 15:7-9 **NIV**

Approach with Assurance

Lesson 21: Persistence - God is never late in answering our prayers.

One of them has grit. The other doesn't know how to quit!

"Hey, Charlie, do you know the difference between perseverance and persistence?"

"What? Is this some kind of joke? Like the one about the teacher asking a student: 'Do you know the difference between ignorance and apathy?' The student replies: 'I don't know and I don't care.' The teacher responds: 'You are right on both counts.'"

"Yah, yah, that's stupid. No, I wasn't telling a joke. The question is from one of my homework assignments. Can you help me out here?"

"Actually, if you really are serious, I can help you with that. Are you up for a bit of a personal story?"

"Sure."

"Well… I showed up for P.E. class one day and the teacher said: 'Today we are going to run the cross-country course. The course is clearly marked so everybody do the best you can and we'll meet you at the finish line.' We didn't really have a choice so off we all went. I figured it was like a day off for him. He holds the timer and we do all the work. It was brutal… 4.5 miles with no chance to train or work our way into shape."

Attribution: Peter van der Sluijs, Creative Commons

"So, what's the point of this story?"

"I'm getting to that. Most of us started off in a jog, but there were some with big egos that had to sprint to the front of the group. I settled into a stride that I thought I could maintain and was determined to keep that pace. It wasn't long before the sprinters had stopped to catch their breath, or couldn't do more than walk. I kept passing one after another because of what some would call perseverance. I simply thought of it as a long-term strategy of never giving up."

"So, you are saying that you were more determined than the others. So… how did you do?"

"I came in second, but the guy who came in first totally ate my lunch. It wasn't even close, but there were about 50 kids that came in behind me. I was able to keep up my pace. Most of my classmates ended up walking up to the finish line. The difference between me and the others was perseverance."

This fictitious example of a teenager is one thing, but in the real world one of the best models for perseverance is the Apostle Paul. He faced many obstacles, dangers and threats, but he pressed on.

Read through 2 Corinthians 6:4-10 NLT. Draw a (circle) around the challenges that would have taken you out of the race. <u>Underline the words</u> that indicate that the Apostle Paul persevered in spite of those obstacles.

Teach Us To Pray | © 2019 | Prayerful Publishing Inc. | www.prayerfulpublishing.com | All Rights Reserved

In everything we do, we show that we are true ministers of God. We patiently endure troubles and hardships and calamities of every kind. We have been beaten, been put in prison, faced angry mobs, worked to exhaustion, endured sleepless nights, and gone without food. We prove ourselves by our purity, our understanding, our patience, our kindness, by the Holy Spirit within us, and by our sincere love. We faithfully preach the truth. God's power is working in us. We use the weapons of righteousness in the right hand for attack and the left hand for defense. We serve God whether people honor us or despise us, whether they slander us or praise us. We are honest, but they call us impostors. We are ignored, even though we are well known. We live close to death, but we are still alive. We have been beaten, but we have not been killed. Our hearts ache, but we always have joy. We are poor, but we give spiritual riches to others. We own nothing, and yet we have everything. – 2 Corinthians 6:4-10 NLT

Which of those challenges would be the most difficult for you to overcome? Why? _____

_____

_____

_____

_____

Perhaps the best example of the Apostle Paul's tenacity and endurance is found in Acts 14:11,19-22. In Lystra God used Paul in the healing of a lame man. At first, they declared that he was a god in human form. Opposition came from neighboring towns, and the next thing you know the mob is stoning him and leaving him for dead. So, what does he do when he regains consciousness? He goes back into town to encourage his fellow believers. He is an amazing example of perseverance.

Let's return to the fictitious example from our teenager. "Thanks for the help with the perseverance thing, but what about *persistence*? Can you help me with this assignment? What's the difference between the two?"

"Unlike perseverance, which is basically pressing on in spite of obstacles, one of the ways *persistence* is defined is: 'to be insistent in the repetition or pressing of a question.' A perseverant person could be called determined, whereas a *persistence* person might be called relentless. "I get it. One of them has grit and the other one is a pest."

"Are you kidding me?! That's your take away from all this? You are only half right. **One of them has grit and the other doesn't know how to quit.** I can see that I'm going to have to use another personal story to help you figure this out. Here goes. My cousin used to tell me about his family and how they prayed for his brother for decades. Everyone in the family had become believers early in life. The only exception was his brother. His brother was the ultimate rebel. In his early teens, he literally antagonized the local police. He rebuffed every effort the family made to help him or share anything about God with him. Nonetheless, the entire family prayed for his salvation on a daily basis. They watched as his life broke down in nearly every way. He went through three failed marriages, another broken relationship, and multiple attempts to overcome his addiction to alcohol. Through all of his struggles, the family *persisted* in their prayers for him. Their prayers won the day. When he finally made his decision for Christ, he didn't talk about it to anyone. He kept it to himself, but the family could see that God was changing him. When his sister finally asked if he had accepted Christ, he answered: "Yes, but he didn't want to say anything because he wasn't sure it would take." **Now that's an outcome that arises from persistent prayer!**

If you want a biblical example, you should look no further than Epaphras. You say you've never heard of him. Well, the Apostle Paul knew about him. Listen to the report he gave about him in Colossians 4:12. NASB *Epaphras, who is one of your number, a bond slave of Jesus Christ, sends you his greetings, always laboring earnestly for you in his prayers, that you may stand perfect and fully assured in all the will of God.* You would be fortunate to have a *persistent* friend like that. I doubt you would call him a pest. So, there is your answer. *Perseverance* (my slogging my way through the cross-country course and The Apostle Paul enduring hardship for the sake of the Kingdom) has grit, and *persistence* (my cousin's family praying for his brother for decades, and Epaphras praying earnestly for their welfare) just won't quit. Get it? Got it? Good!

Now it's time to look at some other sources that can teach us something about *perseverance* and *persistence*. There are multiple quotes and verses to peruse. Reflect on the quality of each of these quotes. Circle one of the following selections and then give your personal opinion by recording why you made that choice.

Quotes on Perseverance and Persistence

"Nothing in the world can take the place of persistence. Talent will not; nothing is more common than unsuccessful men with talent. Genius will not; unrewarded genius is almost a proverb. Education will not; the world is full of educated derelicts. Persistence and determination alone are omnipotent. The slogan Press On! has solved and always will solve the problems of the human race." – Calvin Coolidge

POWERFUL   STRONG   AVERAGE   WEAK

What made you select that adjective? _____

_____

Luke 18:1 NLT One day Jesus told his disciples a story to illustrate their need for constant prayer and to show them that they must never give up. – Luke - A biblical author and doctor

POWERFUL   STRONG   AVERAGE   WEAK

What made you select that adjective? _____

_____

"It's not that I'm so smart, it's just that I stay with problems longer." – Albert Einstein

POWERFUL   STRONG   AVERAGE   WEAK

What made you select that adjective? _____

_____

Psalm 69:13 NLT "But I keep right on praying to you, LORD, hoping this is the time you will show me favor. In your unfailing love, O God, answer my prayer with your sure salvation." – King David

POWERFUL   STRONG   AVERAGE   WEAK

What made you select that adjective? _____

_____

"Perseverance is the hard work you do after you get tired of doing the hard work you already did."
– Newt Gingrich

POWERFUL   STRONG   AVERAGE   WEAK

What made you select that adjective? _____

Colossians 4:2-3 NASB *"Devote yourselves to prayer, keeping alert in it with an attitude of thanksgiving; praying at the same time for us as well, that God will open up to us a door for the word, so that we may speak forth the mystery of Christ, for which I have also been imprisoned."* – Apostle Paul

POWERFUL   STRONG   AVERAGE   WEAK

What made you select that adjective? _____

"Many of life's failures are people who did not realize how close they were to success when they gave up."
– Thomas Edison

POWERFUL   STRONG   AVERAGE   WEAK

What made you select that adjective? _____

Micah 7:7 NIV *"But as for me, I watch in hope for the LORD, I wait for God my Savior; my God will hear me."*
– Prophet Micah

POWERFUL   STRONG   AVERAGE   WEAK

What made you select that adjective? _____

"Making your mark on the world is hard. If it were easy, everybody would do it. But it's not. It takes patience, it takes commitment, and it comes with plenty of failure along the way. The real test is not whether you avoid this failure, because you won't. It's whether you let it harden or shame you into inaction, or whether you learn from it; whether you choose to persevere." – Barack Obama

POWERFUL   STRONG   AVERAGE   WEAK

What made you select that adjective? _____

Galatians 6:9 NIV *"Let us not become weary in doing good, for at the proper time we will reap a harvest if we do not give up."* – Apostle Paul

POWERFUL   STRONG   AVERAGE   WEAK

What made you select that adjective? _____

"Faith is more powerful than government – and nothing is more powerful than God." – Donald Trump

POWERFUL   STRONG   AVERAGE   WEAK

What made you select that adjective? _____

Luke 18:7-8 NIV *"And will not God bring about justice for his chosen ones, who cry out to him day and night? Will he keep putting them off? I tell you, he will see that they get justice, and quickly. However, when the Son of Man comes, will he find faith on the earth?"* – Jesus

POWERFUL   STRONG   AVERAGE   WEAK

What made you select that adjective? _____

"With ordinary talent and extraordinary perseverance, all things are attainable." – Thomas Fowell Buxton

POWERFUL   STRONG   AVERAGE   WEAK

What made you select that adjective? _____

Hebrews 6:11 NIV *"We want each of you to show this same diligence to the very end, so that what you hope for may be fully realized."* – Biblical author, name unknown

POWERFUL   STRONG   AVERAGE   WEAK

What made you select that adjective? _____

"A hero is an ordinary individual who finds strength to persevere and endure in spite of overwhelming obstacles." – Christopher Reeve

POWERFUL   STRONG   AVERAGE   WEAK

What made you select that adjective? _____

Ephesians 6:18 NIV *"And pray in the Spirit on all occasions with all kinds of prayers and requests. With this in mind, be alert and always keep on praying for all the Lord's people."* – Apostle Paul

POWERFUL   STRONG   AVERAGE   WEAK

What made you select that adjective? _____

"Courage and perseverance have a magical talisman, before which difficulties disappear and obstacles vanish into air." – John Quincy Adams

POWERFUL   STRONG   AVERAGE   WEAK

What made you select that adjective? _____

James 1:12 NIV *"Blessed is the one who perseveres under trial because, having stood the test, that person will receive the crown of life that the Lord has promised to those who love him."*
– James, a bond servant of Christ

POWERFUL   STRONG   AVERAGE   WEAK

What made you select that adjective? _____

"Let me tell you the secret that has led to my goal. My strength lies solely in my tenacity." – Louis Pasteur

POWERFUL   STRONG   AVERAGE   WEAK

What made you select that adjective? _____

---

2 Thessalonianss 3:13 NIV *"And as for you, brothers and sisters, never tire of doing what is good."* – Apostle Paul

POWERFUL   STRONG   AVERAGE   WEAK

What made you select that adjective? _____

"If your determination is fixed, I do not counsel you to despair. Few things are impossible to diligence and skill. Great works are performed not by strength, but perseverance." – Samuel Johnson

POWERFUL   STRONG   AVERAGE   WEAK

What made you select that adjective? _____

Psalm 27:14 NLT *"Wait patiently for the LORD. Be brave and courageous. Yes, wait patiently for the LORD."*
– King David

POWERFUL   STRONG   AVERAGE   WEAK

What made you select that adjective? _____

"I am convinced that about half of what separates the successful entrepreneurs from the non-successful ones is pure perseverance." – Steve Jobs

POWERFUL   STRONG   AVERAGE   WEAK

What made you select that adjective? _____

Colossians 1:11-12 NIV *"Being strengthened with all power according to his glorious might so that you may have great endurance and patience, and giving joyful thanks to the Father, who has qualified you to share in the inheritance of his holy people in the kingdom of light."* – Apostle Paul

POWERFUL   STRONG   AVERAGE   WEAK

What made you select that adjective? _____

"If you can't fly then run, if you can't run then walk, if you can't walk then crawl, but whatever you do you have to keep moving forward." – Martin Luther King, Jr.

POWERFUL   STRONG   AVERAGE   WEAK

What made you select that adjective? _____

Acts 1:14 NIV *"They all joined together constantly in prayer, along with the women and Mary the mother of Jesus, and with his brothers."* – Luke - A biblical author and doctor

POWERFUL   STRONG   AVERAGE   WEAK

What made you select that adjective? _____

"The way to succeed is to double your failure rate." – Thomas J. Watson

POWERFUL   STRONG   AVERAGE   WEAK

What made you select that adjective? _____

---

1 Thessalonians 5:17 NLT *"Pray without ceasing."* – Apostle Paul

POWERFUL   STRONG   AVERAGE   WEAK

What made you select that adjective? _____

"Perseverance is a great element of success. If you only knock long enough and loud enough at the gate, you are sure to wake up somebody." – Henry Wadsworth Longfellow

POWERFUL　　STRONG　　AVERAGE　　WEAK

What made you select that adjective? _____

Luke 11:8-9 NASB *"I tell you, even though he will not get up and give him anything because he is his friend, yet because of his persistence he will get up and give him as much as he needs. So I say to you, ask, and it will be given to you; seek, and you will find; knock, and it will be opened to you."* – Jesus

POWERFUL　　STRONG　　AVERAGE　　WEAK

What made you select that adjective? _____

"If you are going through hell, keep going." – Winston Churchill

POWERFUL　　STRONG　　AVERAGE　　WEAK

What made you select that adjective? _____

James 5:11 NLT *"As you know, we count as blessed those who have persevered. You have heard of Job's perseverance and have seen what the Lord finally brought about. The Lord is full of compassion and mercy."*
– James, a bond servant of Christ

POWERFUL　　STRONG　　AVERAGE　　WEAK

What made you select that adjective? _____

"A river cuts through rock, not because of its power, but because of its persistence." – Jim Watkins

POWERFUL　　STRONG　　AVERAGE　　WEAK

What made you select that adjective? _____

Romans 12:12 NIV *"Be joyful in hope, patient in affliction, faithful in prayer."* – Apostle Paul

POWERFUL　　STRONG　　AVERAGE　　WEAK

What made you select that adjective? _____

"Through hard work, perseverance and a faith in God, you can live your dreams." – Ben Carson

POWERFUL   STRONG   AVERAGE   WEAK

What made you select that adjective? _____

Job 17:9 NLT *"The righteous keep moving forward, and those with clean hands become stronger and stronger."* – Job

POWERFUL   STRONG   AVERAGE   WEAK

What made you select that adjective? _____

The short story homework assignment for this and the next lesson is **Improvise 1 & 2**. Read both parts of this story, and then share how *perseverance* was exercised by the following characters in the story.

DAVE: _____

PAUL: _____

BLAIR: _____

Share how *persistence* was exercised by the following characters in the story.

DAVE: _____

PAUL: _____

BLAIR: _____

Circle the word that best describes your efforts to complete this lesson.

ALACRITY   ELAN   CELERITY   ASSIDUITY   SEDULITY   INTREPIDITY

What was it about that particular word that made you select it? _____

- Notes -

Read Lesson 21 Short Story: HHU Vol. 2 - Out of Our Element

- Memory Verse -

"Then He spoke a parable to them, that men always ought to pray and not lose heart, And will not God bring about justice for his chosen ones, who cry out to him day and night? Will he keep putting them off?" Luke 18:1, 7 **NIV**

Approach with Assurance

Lesson 22: Petition/Provision - God knows what you need even before you ask

The answer could be: "No" "Slow" "Grow" or "Go"!

"How do you do that?" "Do what?" "Answer your cell phone before it rings." "My phone is set on a special caller ID mode. It shows the picture of who is calling even before the ringtone sounds." "No way... how did you set that up?" "Well, you have to buy a very special cell phone." "Wow! Where can I get one?" "Actually, I was just messing with you. I do have caller ID set up, but I keep my phone on vibrate. I see who is calling and decide if I want to answer. I leave the ringer off so that other people don't know I'm getting a call." "So, all those times I called and didn't get through, you were simply deciding whether or not you wanted to take my call. Is that how it goes?" "It's kinda like that. Most of the time I really want to hear from you, but when I'm at work or in the midst of a critical conversation, I simply call back at a better time."

"It seems to me that my prayers are working like that. I give God a call, and He gets back to me when He feels like it." "We've talked about this before. God doesn't do that. Sometimes He says 'no,' and you weren't listening or didn't want to hear that. Sometimes He is saying "wait," and He is simply testing your patience and persistence." Someday that whole 'wait and see thing' will be gone forever." "Really? What makes you think that?" "I read about it in Isaiah 65:24 NLT. It says: *"I will answer them before they even call to me. While they are still talking about their needs, I will go ahead and answer their prayers!"* "So, for now, it's coulda, woulda, shoulda, maybe I'll help you." "No, come on. You know better. He has promised to meet our needs. He tells us to ask Him every day for our daily needs. He probably isn't going to provide next year's needs in one day." "Why not?" "Only He knows those answers, but I would guess that He wants us to learn to look to Him and trust Him every day. If He gave us a year's worth in one day, we might blow it all, and then expect the same thing the next day. Or we might say... "I'm rich. What do I need God for?" Solomon summed it up like this in Proverbs 30:7-9 NIV *"Two things I ask of you, LORD; do not refuse me before I die: Keep falsehood and lies far from me; give me neither poverty nor riches, but give me only my daily bread. Otherwise, I may have too much and disown you and say, 'Who is the LORD?' Or I may become poor and steal, and so dishonor the name of my God."*

God knows our needs and has already made provision for them. He has promised to supply everything we need. Philippians 4:19 NIV says: *"But my God shall supply all your needs according to his riches in glory by Christ Jesus."* Let's look at an example of someone making advance preparation for needs that might arise by reviewing the homework for this lesson. In the ***Improvise 1 & 2*** short stories, Dave brought specific items in his attempt to rescue the people in a downed airplane.

58   Teach Us To Pray | © 2019 | Prayerful Publishing Inc. | www.prayerfulpublishing.com | All Rights Reserved

Rescue Provisions Exercise

List some of the items from the *Improvise 1 & 2* stories that Dave chose for the rescue attempt. The CONSONENTS are supplied and the VOWELS are missing in the items we will highlight. These will serve as clues to help you complete the list. In the space that follows, give a short review of why that element was indispensable in Dave's rescue effort.

l_ght s_bst_nt_ _l j_ck_t _____

G_r-T_x c_v_r_lls & gl_v_s _____

m_d_c_l s_ppl_ _s _____

_dv_l / V_c_d_n _____

_ _r spl_nt _____

c_rv_c_l c_ll_r _____

f_ _d _____

c_nn_d m_ _t _____

fr_ _t _____

_n_rgy b_rs _____

w_t_r _____

r_p_ / pl_st_c t_rp _____
_____

_l_ctr_n_c l_c_t_r _____
_____

sm_ll t_nt _____
_____

s_gn_l fl_r_s _____
_____

bl_nk_ts _____
_____

w_rm cl_th_ng _____
_____

h_ _d b_nd w_th L_D l_ght _____
_____

d_ct t_p_ _____
_____

b_n_ s_w _____
_____

L_ _th_rm_n m_lt-t_ _l _____
_____

kn_f_ _____
_____

h_nd g_n _____
_____

Which item was the most vital provision that Dave brought with him? _____

_____

Why did you choose that one? _____

_____

List some of the items from the *Improvise 1 & 2* stories that Paul and Blair brought that aided in their rescue. The CONSONENTS are supplied and the VOWELS are missing in the items we will highlight. These will serve as clues to help you complete the list. In the space that follows, give a short review of why that element was indispensable in the rescue effort.

b_kl_v_ _____

_____

r_bb_r c_ _t _____

_____

r_bb_r p_nts _____

_____

t_ _q_ _ _____

_____

sl_ _p_ng b_gs _____

_____

Which item was the most vital provision that Paul and Blair brought with them? _____

_____

Why did you choose that one? _____

_____

List some of the items from the *Improvise 1 & 2* stories that were in the plane (or part of the plane) that were helpful in the rescue attempt. The CONSONENTS are supplied and the VOWELS are missing in the items we will highlight. These will serve as clues to help you complete the list. In the space that follows, give a short review of why that element was indispensable in Dave's rescue effort.

s_ _ts _f th_ _ _rpl_ne _____

_____

Teach Us To Pray I © 2019 I Prayerful Publishing Inc. I www.prayerfulpublishing.com I All Rights Reserved

w_ng _f th_ pl_n_ _____

_____

s_ _t b_lts _____

_____

w_ _l bl_nk_ts _____

_____

l_ _s_ b_gg_g_ _____

_____

tr_nsm_tt_r b_ _c_n _____

_____

Which item in the plane (or part of the plane) was the most vital element of this rescue? _____

_____

Why did you choose that one? _____

_____

    List some ways that a gust of wind may have assisted the rescue efforts. The CONSONENTS are supplied and the VOWELS are missing in the items we will highlight. These will serve as clues to help you complete the list. In the space that follows, give a short review of why that element was indispensable in Dave's rescue effort.

ch_ng_d p_s_t_ _n _f th_ pl_n_ _____

_____

br_ _ght b_tt_ry b_ck t_ l_f_ _____

_____

m_d_ _x_t _ _s_ _r _____

_____

pr_v_d_d _ns_l_t_ _n _____

_____

pr_t_ct_d p_l_t's b_dy fr_m pr_d_t_rs _____

_____

– Reflection Point –

Written in the front page of Dr. David Jeremiah's Bible:
*When you pray, if the **REQUEST** is wrong, God says: **"NO."***
*When you pray, if the **TIMING** is wrong, God says: **"SLOW."***
*When you pray, if you need to **FIX SOMETHING IN YOUR LIFE**, God says: **"GROW."***
*If the **REQUEST** is right, and the **TIMING** is right, and **YOU** are right, God says: **"GO!"***

Choose from the four possible answers to prayer listed in the **Reflection Point** above. Read the passages that are listed below, and assign which word would best describe God's answer to that person's request. Select from these choices: **WRONG REQUEST – TIMING'S NOT RIGHT – FIX SOMETHING – YOU GOT IT**. It is possible that more than one selection could be correct.

Acts 16:6-14, Acts 19:21-22, 2 Corinthians 1:15-20 **Paul** _____

Matthew 17:14-21 **Disciples** _____

1 Chronicles 28:2-6, 29:10-19 **David** _____

Esther 3:13-5:8, 6:14-7:6 **Esther** _____

Judges 6:11-16, 36-40; 7:2-14 **Gideon** _____

Deuteronomy 3:23-28 **Moses** _____

1 Samuel 23:1-5, 2 Samuel 5:17-25 **David** _____

Luke 2:25-38 **Simeon, Anna** _____

Can you think of some of your prayers about which God said: *WRONG REQUEST?* _____
_____

Can you think of some of your prayers about which God said: *TIMING'S NOT RIGHT?* _____
_____

Can you think of some prayers about which God said: *FIX SOMETHING?* _____
_____

Can you think of some prayers about which God said: *YOU GOT IT?* _____
_____

Read Lesson 22 Short Story: HHU Vol. 1 - Improvise Part 1

– Memory Verse –

Don't worry about anything; instead, pray about everything. Tell God what you need, and thank him for all he has done.
Philippians 4:6 NLT

Approach with Assurance

Lesson 23: Shelter - Protection from the Storms of Life

Why does that person have to be such a bully?

"Did you read what she said about her on Facebook?" "Do you think that it could possibly be true?" her friend replied. "I don't know why that person has to be such a bully!"

Now, there's a great place to start. **Why does that person have to be such a bully?**

Have you ever considered some of the improper motivations behind their behavior? When you contrast those motivations with the characteristics of love described in 1 Corinthians 13, you might begin to see what is really at work.

> Love is patient, love is kind and is not jealous; love does not brag and is not arrogant, does not act unbecomingly; it does not seek its own, is not provoked, does not take into account a wrong *suffered*, does not rejoice in unrighteousness, but rejoices with the truth; bears all things, believes all things, hopes all things, endures all things. Love never fails.
>
> **1 Corinthians 13:4-8 NASB**

LOVE vs. Bullying/Abuse

Write down words that describe the opposite or an absence of love in the space provided below.

LOVE is patient	Bullying/Abuse is _____
LOVE is kind	Bullying/Abuse is _____
LOVE is not jealous	Bullying/Abuse is _____
LOVE does not brag	Bullying/Abuse is **not** _____
LOVE is not arrogant	Bullying/Abuse is _____
LOVE does not act unbecomingly	Bullying/Abuse is **not** _____
LOVE does not seek its own	Bullying/Abuse is _____
LOVE is not provoked	Bullying/Abuse **does not** _____
LOVE does not take into account a wrong *suffered*	Bullying/Abuse is _____
LOVE does not rejoice in unrighteousness	Bullying/Abuse is _____
LOVE rejoices with the truth	Bullying/Abuse is _____
LOVE bears all things	Bullying/Abuse is _____
LOVE believes all things	Bullying/Abuse _____ all things
LOVE hopes all things	Bullying/Abuse _____ all things
LOVE endures all things	Bullying/Abuse _____ all things

    The *love motivation is the ideal for us* on the personal level. There are other motivations and responsibilities in response to bullying/abuse. The motivation to protect the abused is a correct response for you, for friends, for authorities and others. Finding a way to withdraw (seek shelter) from a bullying or abusive situation is generally a good start. That is not always possible or easily done. A person and/or an agency may be able to find a reasonable means of confronting the destructive behavior. Choosing to appeal to a person of authority as a potential means of support (both personal and legal) is also an option.

    While there are many options available, we should always realize that our best refuge and first choice is God! **We can call out to Him for shelter, protection, justice and support.** Ask Him to make Psalm 12:5 a reality in your circumstance. We can pray that God might intervene for us, for the perpetrator, and any others who might be involved in the situation.

Bullying/Abuse Word Puzzle

Bullying and abuse are very similar in nature. We will learn that these abusive situations are always wrong, but it appears that even good people have been subjected to such things. To suffer from these kinds of experiences is not something God desires for us, but a horrible expression of a sinful humanity. Obviously, there was no cyber-bullying in Scriptural time, but we will use harassment as an illustration. See if you can find the following 9 abuse categories, and then match them to the examples found in the Scriptures that follow. They are VERBAL, PHYSICAL, RACIAL, CHILD, CYBER, SIBLING, POWER, SEXUAL and SPOUSAL.

S	P	O	U	S	A	L	Z	G	H	S	G	R	U	I
V	X	P	J	X	P	P	N	K	E	Y	B	E	M	F
M	E	A	K	L	H	I	L	X	D	S	W	W	S	Z
V	R	R	H	S	L	U	U	O	Q	L	A	O	S	I
A	Y	Y	B	B	X	A	Q	K	X	F	I	P	L	D
L	U	Q	I	A	L	D	R	E	B	Y	C	H	L	W
A	M	S	M	Q	L	T	Z	X	E	D	C	Z	C	R
C	R	P	E	U	R	U	F	W	W	W	Y	Z	S	B
I	A	U	U	V	N	D	T	G	Q	A	P	K	G	Y
S	C	R	U	K	X	W	L	E	S	K	B	U	Q	I
Y	I	D	D	G	Y	J	H	I	N	O	K	J	J	G
H	A	Y	D	C	F	Z	L	C	T	X	F	J	L	H
P	L	V	O	D	Z	U	A	B	N	J	P	J	W	Y
F	S	F	A	A	K	B	B	N	K	S	D	E	Y	Y
E	D	C	T	E	G	V	P	T	J	D	V	B	X	N

Match a type of abuse/bullying found in the word puzzle with the following Scriptures. Based on what we learned from I Corinthians 13, what would your prayer or course of action look like in this scriptural example? How did God respond, or *how would God likely respond* in those situations? Some catagories will fit in more than one example.

Luke 11:14-22; 12:1-7 for example VERBAL or POWER

Prayer for or action towards the abuser. _____
_____

Prayer for or action towards the person who is abused. _____
_____

What are some of God's responses to the bullying/abuse? _____
_____

Genesis 12:11-19 _____

Prayer for or action towards the abuser. _____
_____

Prayer for or action towards the person who is abused. _____
_____

What are some of God's responses to the bullying/abuse? _____
_____

Mark 14:32-36, 64-65; Luke 23:33-34 _____

Prayer for or action towards the abuser. _____
_____

Prayer for or action towards the person who is abused. _____
_____

What are some of God's responses to the bullying/abuse? _____
_____

John 4:4, 9-10, 25-29 _____

Prayer for or action towards the abuser. _____
_____

Prayer for or action towards the person who is abused. _____
_____

What are some of God's responses to the bullying/abuse? _____
_____

1 Samuel 1:6-7, 10, 15-18 _____

    Prayer for or action towards the abuser. _____

    Prayer for or action towards the person who is abused. _____

    What are some of God's responses to the bullying/abuse? _____

Genesis 37:18-24, 28-29; 39:1-5, 21; 40:14-15; 42:6-8, 28, 31-34; 50:20-21 _____

    Prayer for or action towards the abuser. _____

    Prayer for or action towards the person who is abused. _____

    What are some of God's responses to the bullying/abuse? _____

2 Samuel 13:11-12, 20-21; 18:14-15, 33 _____

    Prayer for or action towards the abuser. _____

    Prayer for or action towards the person who is abused. _____

    What are some of God's responses to the bullying/abuse? _____

1 Samuel 19:1-2, 10-12, 18; 20:15-17; 23:16; 2 Samuel 5:1-4 _____

    Prayer for or action towards the abuser. _____

    Prayer for or action towards the person who is abused. _____

    What are some of God's responses to the bullying/abuse? _____

2 Samuel 11:1-5; 12:7-13, 24-25 _____

Prayer for or action towards the abuser. _____
_____

Prayer for or action towards the person who is abused. _____
_____

What are some of God's responses to the bullying/abuse? _____
_____

- Notes -

_____
_____
_____
_____
_____
_____
_____
_____
_____

Read Lesson 22 Short Story: HHU Vol. 1 - Improvise Part 2

- Memory Verse -

He will rescue us because you are helping by praying for us. As a result, many will give thanks to God because so many people's prayers for our safety have been answered.
2 Corinthians 1:11 **NLT**

Approach with Compassion

Lesson 24: Mercy - His mercies never fail

It's not my list. It's God's list.

"I said: Sit up straight... I've told you a million times not to slouch."

"OK, Mom. I'm finally going to say it: 'Why should I care?'"

"I anticipated that question, and you might be surprised to know that there are good reasons for you to sit up straight. Erik Peper, in a 2003 Ohio State University study, found the following:

1. According to this experiment, when we sit up straight, we are more likely to remember positive memories or think of something positive in general.

2. Another insight was that if we skip during breaks, we can significantly increase our energy levels. On the other hand, a slow, slumped walk can do the exact opposite and drain us of our energy.

3. The study also found that those who slouched before the study found their energy drained more than others and were most affected by depression."

"It's your constant nagging on me that's draining my energy. Why don't you give me a break and focus on something that might one day truly be important?"

"You could be right. I get your point. There are more important things than your posture. How about if I narrow my nagging down to three simple points?

1. Try to be fair to people all the time.
2. Be kind to everyone, and
3. Help others feel very special."

"That sounds good. Where did you come up with that list?"

"**It's not my list. It's God's list.** In Micah 6:8 God said this: *He has shown you, O man, what is good; and what does the LORD require of you but to do justly, to love mercy, and to walk humbly with your God?*" NKJV

"Basically, you are telling me to be like Jesus. Is that right?"

"Well, more like I'm asking you to let God help you move in that direction. For instance, I'm asking you to be kinder to your little sister. I know that God would have to help you with that, but that's what Jesus would do."

"So, where do you find that Mom?"

"I'm glad you asked. You'll find it in the book of Luke. Jesus showed mercy to every person who asked for mercy, and even some who didn't. Let's thumb our way through each chapter for examples of mercy.

"To make it more interesting, I've made it into a crossword puzzle for you. Simply consider this as a case study in how God treats us, and how He wants us to treat others. If you are looking for motivation for doing this study, simply read Hebrews 4:16: *Let us therefore come boldly to the throne of grace, that we may obtain mercy and find grace to help in time of need.* NKJV If you want my revised Mom's version... *if want God to listen to you when you ask Him for help, maybe you should be kind to your little sister. I'll help you out by giving you four free ones.*"

"THANKS MOM... I love crossword puzzles!"

Mercy Crossword Puzzle

Find the key word, person or place where mercy was demonstrated in the book of Luke.
Use the NKJV for this exercise.

ACROSS
- 2. Luke 17:11-15
- 6. Luke 3:2-6
- 8. Luke 20:1-8
- 10. Luke 24:44-49
- 11. Luke 10:33-37
- 12. Luke 15:20-24
- 15. Luke 6:35-36
- 17. Luke 9:52-56
- 18. Luke 19:1-10
- 19. Luke 8:36-39
- 20. Luke 11:1-4, 13
- 23. Luke 1:11-14, 18, 57-58
- 24. Luke 16:19-25

DOWN
- 1. Luke 21:12-15
- 3. Luke 14:21-24
- 4. Luke 2:25-31
- 5. Luke 7:2-10
- 7. Luke 12:27-32
- 9. Luke 23:39-43
- 13. Luke 5:8
- 14. Luke 18:38-43; Mark 10:46-52
- 16. Luke 4:16-21
- 21. Luke 13:10-13, 16
- 22. Luke 22:48-51

Filled answers shown: 8 Across: SCRIBES; 17 Across: SAMARITANS; 16 Down: NAZARETH; 24 Across: LAZARUS

We all want to be more like Jesus and one of the best ways that we can do this is by showing mercy to people in need. How many ways can you demonstrate mercy in someone's life in the coming week? _____

_____
_____
_____
_____
_____

- Notes -

Read Lesson 24 Short Story: HHU Vol. 2 - Searching For Paradise II

- Memory Verse -

Let us therefore come boldly unto the throne of grace, that we may obtain mercy, and find grace to help in time of need.

Hebrews 4:16 **NKJV**

Approach with Compassion

Lesson 25: Forgive - When you stand praying, forgive

It's not like you have an an option here!

"It's not like you have an option here."

"You don't understand! It's already hurting a lot, and you are telling me that it's going to hurt even more when you set it? Have you ever had a broken bone, Doc?"

"If you refuse to do this… you are going to have to deal with even more pain. Yes, this is going to hurt, but let me tell you what's going to happen if I don't set this bone. It will likely create stress fractures which tend to increase in severity until the pain becomes disabling. Over time, if left untreated, a stress fracture can put you at risk of suffering an additional fracture in that bone. In other words, you are likely to have this same bone break again. Now, is that what you really want?"

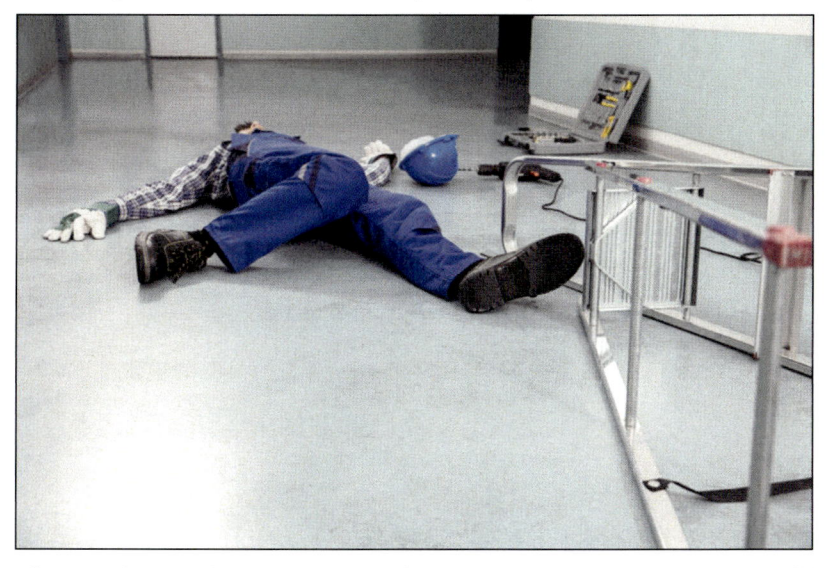

"I didn't want any of this! I didn't want a broken leg, and I sure didn't want to come to the hospital."

"What you wanted in this case is irrelevant. This leg has a compound fracture. If we set this bone properly, it could be stronger when it gets fully healed. Are you ready?"

"Augghhhh!! I guess I'm supposed to say, 'Thanks, Doc.' Let me tell you, I'm not in the mood to hand out compliments."

"You'll be thanking me later. You are going to have to wear a cast for a little while to protect it and keep it in place."

Our hearts can be broken too. We must ultimately get them properly aligned, or they won't heal. We'll have to give them a protective shell for a time, but not forever. You wouldn't want to wear a cast on your leg for the rest of your life, would you? Yet, after some people have been hurt, they never let their guard down again. They never take away the protective shell. Sure, we must make certain that we try to avoid the kind of thing that led to that "break," but a closed heart isn't going to lead to a healthy life.

Forgiveness is a step towards healing your broken heart. That's one of the reasons Jesus said: *"If you don't forgive, you won't be forgiven."* The other person needs your forgiveness so they can heal and live in freedom, but so do you. God wants all of us to live an abundant life, and we just can't do that when we carry the baggage of a cast around our hearts.

Today, we are going to look at some of the critical elements in the topic of **forgiveness**. It is vital to our relationship with God and with others. It is critical to our personal and spiritual health. So, let's dig in. Let's be prepared to face some short-term pain for the sake of a better outcome. Let's do the hard work that leads to a better life!

Be forewarned. If you think that forgiveness comes without some pain or personal cost, you will likely be disappointed. Just like the resetting of a broken leg, there may be some pain in the healing process. It would be great if everything could be remedied through a simple "**I'm sorry,**" or "**Please, forgive me,**" or "**I was wrong.**" Those short, simple phrases are often fired off without the depth of meaning and commitment which they demand.

Think of the cost of the forgiveness that Jesus brought into your life. **It wasn't cheap.** Even a cursory examination of the price He paid shows us how costly it was for Him. If you would like to envision the cost of forgiveness which will be talked about in this lesson, go to YouTube and find the two-minute trailer of the movie **The Passion of the Christ**. Following that trailer, reflect on these words of Paul in Colossians 3:13: *"Make allowance for each other's faults, and forgive anyone who offends you. Remember, the Lord forgave you, so you must forgive others."* NLT

Just like the resetting of a broken bone, the cost of forgiving others can be very real. The impact of not forgiving others can be even more costly… for them and for us. There is no need to be afraid, but be prepared to grow through pain. ***Jesus has been there, and He will walk with you through this challenge.*** He won't take us anywhere He hasn't already gone, and in the end, there will be healing all around. Thank God for His indescribable gift!

There are a host of passages that speak clearly on this issue. Today, we are going to focus three of them through something we call the **Forgiveness Ladder**. We will do an overview of Psalm 51, Matthew 18:21-35 and Luke 7:36-50. Ladders can be tricky and sometimes dangerous things. Yes, they can take you to new heights, but watch your footing or you will regret the landing. If you don't forgive, you'll end up going back to the place where you will need to seek His mercy. You won't reach those new heights without moving up the ladder!

The Forgiveness Ladder

Review each passage and write the portion you select in the light green area left of the step on the **Forgiveness Ladder**. Some of the selected portions may match in more than one category. **Some scriptural passages may not include every step on the ladder.** We'll give you the example of the bottom step.

You cannot take any steps up the ladder *with unforgiveness in your heart*. Trying to do so would result in the need go back to Step One.

Psalm 51:10-13   Psalm 51:18-19   Psalm 51:1-4   Psalm 51:5-9   Psalm 51:14-17

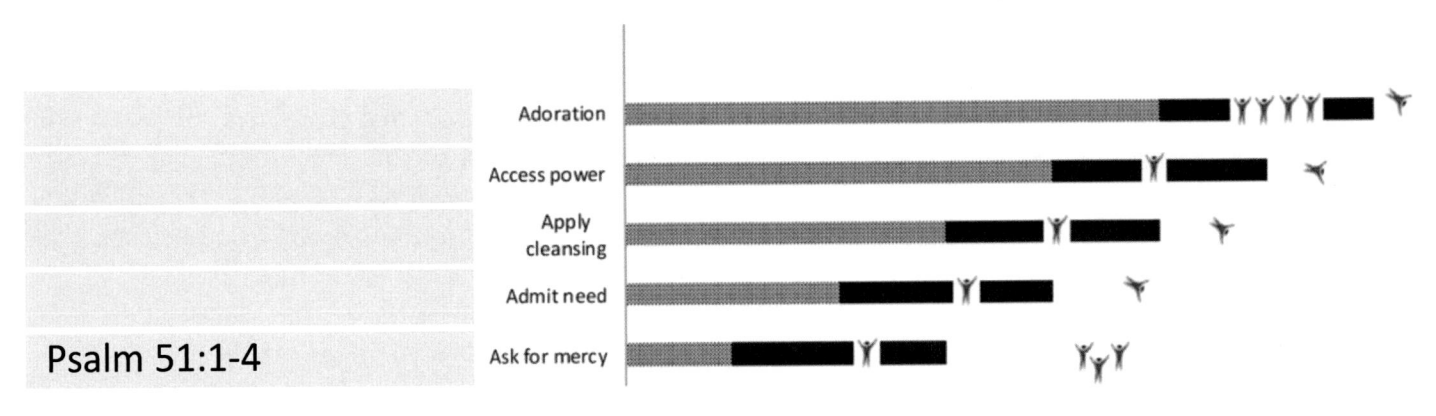

Ladder steps (bottom to top):
- Ask for mercy — *Psalm 51:1-4*
- Admit need
- Apply cleansing
- Access power
- Adoration

What is the likely condition (results) of a person with a serious compound fracture who refused to admit that they have something that needs to be done to improve their condition? _____

Matthew 18:31-33   Matthew 18:34-35   Matthew 18:21-26   Matthew 18:27-30

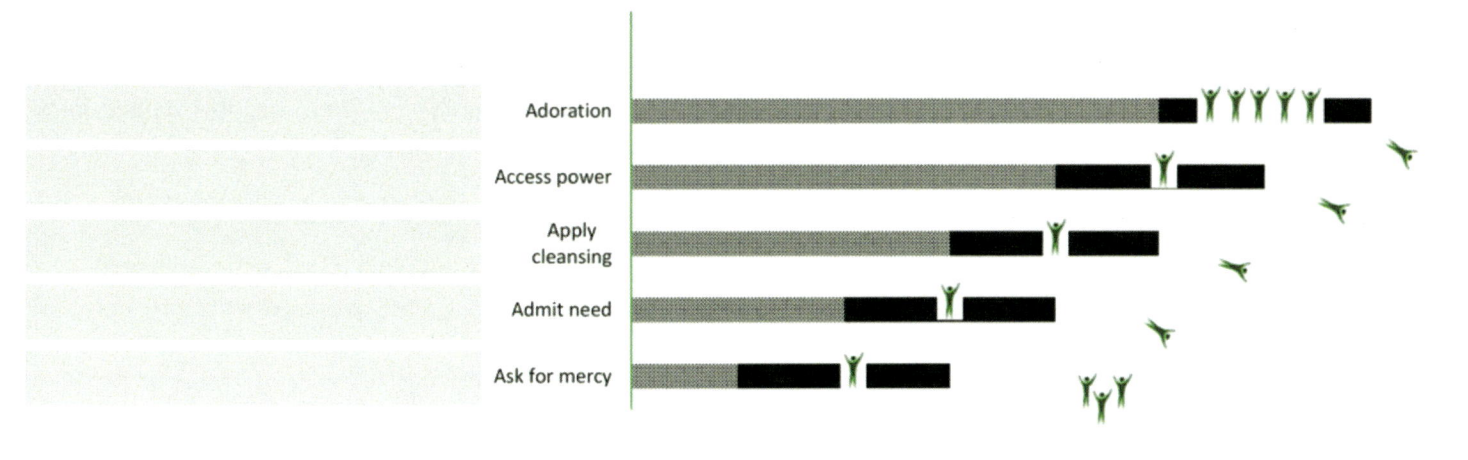

What is the likely condition of the person who refuses to apply cleansing to their wound? _____
_____
_____
_____

Luke:7:36-38   Luke 7:44-46   Luke 7:47-48   Luke 7:39-43   Luke 7:49-50

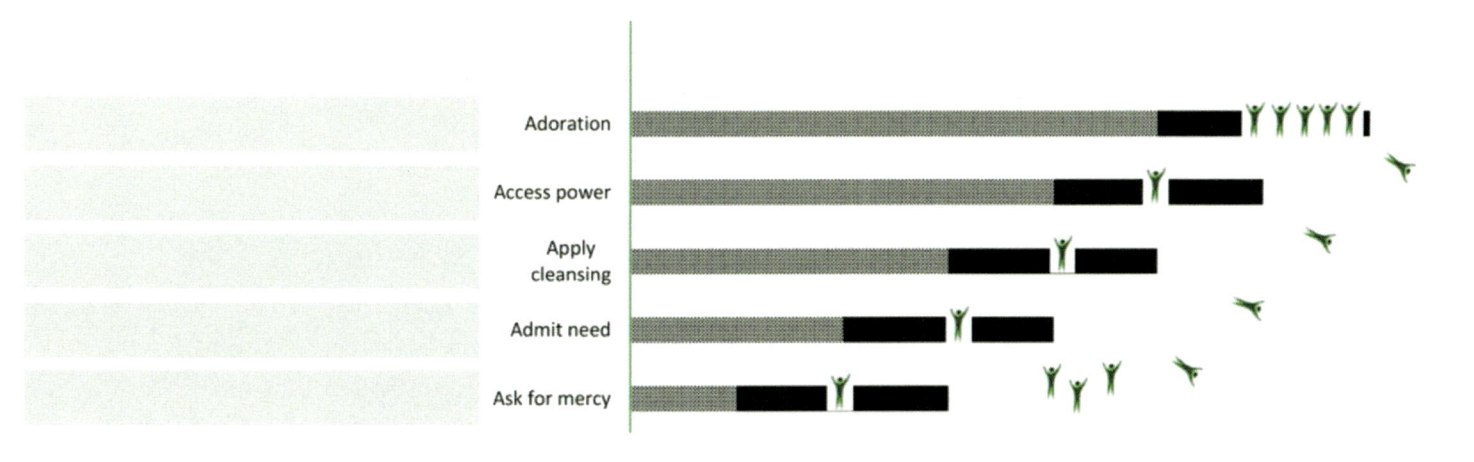

Most of us are at different points in the forgiveness ladder at certain points in our lives. Where would you say that you are at today? Do you want to move to the next level, or are you happy where you are? _____
_____
_____
_____

Read Lesson 25 Short Story: HHU Vol. 1 - Small Minded

"Not An Option" Matching Exercise

For this next exercise, draw a line from the scripture reference to the correct verse(s). This can be found in this week's **Prayer Prompts** homework assignment.

Mark 11:25-26	Therefore, if you bring your gift to the altar, and there remember that your brother has something against you, leave your gift there before the altar, and go your way. First be reconciled to your brother, and then come and offer your gift. NKJV
Romans 12:20	"But I say to you who hear, love your enemies, do good to those who hate you, bless those who curse you, pray for those who mistreat you." NIV
1 John 1:9	Instead, do what the Scriptures say: "If your enemies are hungry, feed them. If they are thirsty, give them something to drink, and they will be ashamed of what they have done to you." NLT
Matthew 5:23-24	If we confess our sins, he is faithful and just and will forgive us our sins and purify us from all unrighteousness. NIV
Luke 6:27-28	"And whenever you stand praying, if you have anything against anyone, forgive him, that your Father in heaven may also forgive you your trespasses. But if you do not forgive, neither will your Father in heaven forgive your trespasses." NKJV

- Notes -

___

- Memory Verse -

And be kind to one another, tenderhearted, forgiving one another, even as God in Christ forgave you.
Ephesians 4:32 NKJV

Prayer Prompts Calendar

NOW AVAILABLE for your favorite device...
FREE for Apple devices from The App Store and
FREE for Android devices at Google Play.

Providing Biblical Tools to Support Your Christian Walk

PRAYERFUL PUBLISHING

Teach us to Pray

Unit Contents:

UNIT 1: Transcendent Kingdom – *Introduction*
- Lesson 1: Pray in this way
- Lesson 2: Diligently search for Him

UNIT 2: Transcendent Kingdom – *Approach with Awe*
- Lesson 3: Creator of heaven and earth
- Lesson 4: The God of Holiness
- Lesson 5: The God of Love
- Lesson 6: The God of Righteousness

UNIT 3: Transcendent Kingdom – *Approach with Reverence*
- Lesson 7: Worship in Spirit and Truth
- Lesson 8: Praying "in Jesus name" means
- Lesson 9: Praying "in Jesus name" doesn't mean
- Lesson 10: What "Spirit led" prayer means
- Lesson 11: What "Spirit led" prayer doesn't mean
- Lesson 12: Praying "in Truth"

UNIT 4: Kingdom Builders – *Approach with Meekness*
- Lesson 13: Gratitude
- Lesson 14: Humility
- Lesson 15: Grace
- Lesson 16: Faith
- Lesson 17: Joy

UNIT 5: Kingdom Builders – *Approach with Devotion*
- Lesson 18: Fellowship
- Lesson 19: Submission
- Lesson 20: Abiding

UNIT 6: Kingdom Builders – *Approach with Assurance*
- Lesson 21: Persistence
- Lesson 22: Petition/Provision
- Lesson 23: Shelter

UNIT 7: Kingdom Builders – *Approach with Compassion*
- Lesson 24: Mercy
- Lesson 25: Forgiveness

UNIT 8: Kingdoms in Conflict – *Approach with Confidence*
- Lesson 26: Temptation
- Lesson 27: Armour of God
- Lesson 28: Fortress
- Lesson 29: Intercession
- Lesson 30: The defeated Enemy
- Lesson 31: Unending battle... ultimate victory
- Lesson 32: It is written

UNIT 9: Kingdoms in Conflict – *Approach with Anticipation*
- Lesson 33: God's Kingdom
- Lesson 34: God's Power
- Lesson 35: God's Glory

Made in the USA
Middletown, DE
23 June 2023